Bitter Rose
and
Three Storey, Ocean View

Bitter Rose
and
Three Storey, Ocean View

Catherine Banks

Bitter Rose and Three Storey, Ocean View
first published 2014 by
Scirocco Drama
An imprint of J. Gordon Shillingford Publishing Inc.
© 2014 Catherine Banks

Scirocco Drama Editor: Glenda MacFarlane
Cover design by Terry Gallagher/Doowah Design Inc.
Cover artwork by Karen Klee-Atkin
Author photo by Heidi Hamilton
Printed and bound in Canada on 100% post-consumer recycled paper.

We acknowledge the financial support of the Manitoba Arts Council and The Canada
Council for the Arts for our publishing program.

Library and Archives Canada Cataloguing in Publication

Banks, Catherine, 1957-
[Plays. Selection]
    Bitter rose and Three storey, ocean view / Catherine Banks.

Plays.
Contents: Bitter rose–Three storey, ocean view
ISBN 978-1-927922-05-7 (pbk.)

    I. Title.

PS8553.A5635A6 2014   C812'.54   C2014-905820-9

J. Gordon Shillingford Publishing
P.O. Box 86, RPO Corydon Avenue, Winnipeg, MB Canada R3M 3S3

BITTER ROSE

Catherine Banks

Catherine Banks' plays include *It is Solved by Walking, Bone Cage, Three Storey, Ocean View, Bitter Rose* and *The Summer of the Piping Plover*. *Bitter Rose* aired on Bravo! Canada. *Bone Cage* won the Governor General's Literary Award for Drama in 2008 and *It is Solved by Walking* won the GG in 2012.

Banks' plays are characterized by black humour, and compelling dramatic metaphor. *It is Solved by Walking* has been translated into Catalan by Tant per Tant and was one of three Canadian plays that toured Catalonia in November, 2012.

This play is dedicated to Leah Benvie Hamilton
who listened and listened and listened.

Acknowledgements

Tessa Mendel and Marina Endicott were instrumental in the development of *Bitter Rose* and *Three Storey, Ocean View*. Their gentle, insightful feedback and unfailing support gor me through some very difficult times.

Thanks to my ever-patient children Rilla and Simon.

Thank-you Karen Klee-Atlin for creating a beautiful print for the cover.

I'm very grateful to Gordon Shillingford for publishing these plays and for Glenda MacFarlane's insightful editing. This publication means the world to me.

Production History

Bitter Rose had its premiere at Du Maurier Theatre (Neptune), Halifax, on November 15, 2000, with the following cast:

ROSE .... Amy House

Directed by Tessa Mendel
Set Design by Bill Forbes
Lighting Design by Leigh Ann Vardy
Costume Design by Karin Jones
Sound / Photography by Terry Pulliam
Stage Manager: Seana McCrodan

Bitter Rose had a workshop / production at LSPU Hall, St. John's, NL, in August, 1999, with the following cast:

ROSE .... Amy House

Directed by Michael Chiasson

Bitter Rose was developed with the assistance of The Canada Council for the Arts, The Nova Scotia Arts Council, The Women's Theatre and Creativity Centre, LSPU HALL (St. John's) and Playwright's Atlantic Resource Centre's Trinity Bay Workshop '97, dramaturg Janis Spence. *Bitter Rose* aired on Bravo Canada! in 2005 as part of the Singular Series.

The playwright wishes to thank Ruth Lawrence, Paula Danckert, Marina Endicott, Tessa Mendel, Lois Brown, Michael Chiasson, Mary Vingoe, Laura MacLauchlan, Leah Hamilton, Lenora Steele and Karen Klee-Atlin and the very funny and brave Amy House. I most especially want to honour the wonderful late Janis Spence who read the first draft and said, "It's not bitter enough." I am deeply grateful for those words and for the beacon of light, Janis' artistry, that continues to shine through those of us who were lucky enough to have worked with her.

Playwrights Note

The stage directions for *Bitter Rose* given here are really bare bones thoughts towards stage directions. Except where the script dictates an action, the director, together with the actor and designer are free to imagine Rose's physical world. One director may wish to use slides or video, another a representational set, another a bare stage and a stool.

Act I

The basement rec room of a middle-class family. Aside from the usual things such as a sofa, chair, maybe a TV, there is on the wall a huge blank canvas (this serves as a projection screen) and a workbench with tole painting supplies as well as artist paints and brushes.

ROSE enters. She is dressed in her wedding dress and veil. There are bloodstains on the dress, one on her shoulder, one on her right breast and one in her lap. Pinned over her left breast is a large heart made of construction paper that reads VOLUNTEER MOM.

ROSE is carrying two grocery bags. She puts the bags down, takes out a rumpled newspaper and begins to spread it over the floor.

ROSE: I read the obituaries this morning. I always do. Well, not all of them, but the ones that are in my age group. Not that I'm comparing myself to what they accomplished...well actually that is what I'm doing.

This one this morning really got me down. It said, Rhonda Brown, 46, daughter of, wife of, mother to etc...and then: *She was an avid walker.* Just like that, those exact words. *She was an avid walker.* And I thought, Jesus, what have I been doing?

ROSE stands back, makes several adjustments to the papers. Her eyes are pulled to the blank canvas on the wall. She walks over, staring at it, then turns away. She turns back immediately and turns the blank surface to the wall.

Don't you just love the power of a wedding dress?

She turns to the audience and continues a slow turning like a child showing off her Sunday best.

I don't care who you are, you see a woman in a long white dress, you notice her right off. Right away. And if she's coming out of the church you slow down to have a good look. Everybody does.

When I see a woman in a white dress the first thing I wonder is, did she keep her own name? I can't help it; it just pops into my head. Did she keep her own name? Not that it matters. Like my mother used to say, "You're tarred with the same brush."

ROSE unpacks baby food jars and baby wipes from the grocery bags.

A wedding dress is highly symbolic. If you don't think so take a look at Bill's face, he's my husband, when he walks in and sees that I am in my wedding dress. By now the university librarian has called him, the manager of the IGA too and the supervisor of the school lunch program.

ROSE fingers the heart on her dress.

Lately, well around me, he looks like that horse in Alex Colville's painting, like he's charging full gallop towards an oncoming freight train, and not sure that jumping to the left or right will save himself. Saving himself might be to take the full impact and be put out of his misery at last. His eyes say, "If only I could be sure I wouldn't survive."

The phone rings three times, stops. ROSE carefully lays out the paintbrushes.

I don't blame him really. He's got to strap on his wooden leg every morning and face distraught students, an overwrought faculty, and President Bob.

ROSE does a little limping walk around. She stops, grinning.

Of course it's a symbolic missing leg. Every tenured professor has one, according to the definition of a full professor. It's not a clean, healed amputation they require, either. No, it's a ragged, festering, bloody stump.

She begins to open the baby food jars in front of her. There are peas, beef and orange squash.

I don't want you to think I couldn't have made my own way in the world. I have my BA. We were discussing this at our last tole painting morning. Well, the whole bunch of us in the group have our BAs. Except for the instructor, Gerta. She got her GED last year. Gerta can paint circles around us. She doesn't have that damn Art History 101 screwing with her head like the rest of us. No I want to tell you I was going places, or saving money to go places. Then there was falling in love, marriage and kids and falling behind, and suddenly I'm getting up in the morning and scaring the shit out of Bill and myself too.

ROSE dips a brush in the squash jar and sucks it clean.

These are not the shoes that came with the dress... these red ones. I wear them because they remind me I'm 43, and I'm not in Kansas any more.

Now when I was home, back in Kansas...yes, really... Well, Kansas as a state of mind.

ROSE goes back to the floor and kneels down spreading the dress out before her. She is selecting brushes and putting them carefully in the baby-food jars.

When I was twenty, back when things were black or white, I wasn't going to change the world. My idea was to hold up huge reflecting mirrors, paint huge canvases showing exactly what everyone in the world was like on the inside.

I was trying to describe this idea to Gerta one day last week. Gerta has become mother confessor of our group. She does such a beautiful job talking down our playwright, who gets suicidal every year at this time when the theatres are announcing their seasons. She asked me, "How much would a really large canvas of people's insides sell for?" She thinks maybe there isn't the market for it like there would have been twenty years ago. That's OK, the details of the paintings are a bit fuzzy, anyway. I'm not blaming that on anyone either. And I'm not going to make a joke about early onset Alzheimers.

ROSE begins to paint on her dress with baby food. She concentrates; she wants to get it right.

When Susan was a baby I would sometimes use her baby food to create miniatures on the highchair tray. Miniatures of the huge paintings I planned to create...some day. I couldn't be stopped! I created these pureed pea, squash and beef masterpieces.

She stands showing off the wonderful painting she just created.

Yum yum.

Pause.

NO. No I didn't. That's something I made up once as something I would say after I was famous and a biographer asked me about those lost years...1994 to well—now I guess.

Have you ever seen the Warhol painting of Marilyn Monroe? Twenty-five squares filled with twenty-five faces of Marilyn Monroe. He was playing with the idea that everyone achieves fifteen minutes of Fame except for Marilyn got more...25 minutes.

That got me thinking about adding up my minutes of fame. Not big Marilyn minutes, not international stardom, nothing like that. Just, you know, the times that for a minute I was in the centre of some teeny-tiny spotlight.

A projector light appears on the blank canvas.

As ROSE announces her name a picture appears of ROSE at 12 in cats-eye glasses.

Rose, Grade Seven, Third Prize in Fire Prevention Week Slogan Contest. "Sing this land is ours and keep it that way, don't let forest fires take it away..."

A slide of fifteen-year-old ROSE, in a cardboard and foil crown in the next square.

Rose, Grade Nine, Miss Winter Carnival.

A slide of ROSE at 17, holding a painting proudly.

Rose, Grade Twelve, Painting "Sweet Puppy Dead on the Road" shown in a national exhibition of art by promising students.

The slide projector clicks but next slides are blank.

Rose, 25, has a two-headed baby.

Rose, 30, sells children to buy art supplies.

Rose, 39, found missing.

ROSE shakes herself out.

No, that's it.

Just three squares of fame.

ROSE begins to clean up the mess. She wipes off the excess food with the baby wipes and closes up the jars.

Doesn't everyone want to make a mark in the world, be remembered through history, leave something that lasts fifty, one hundred, three hundred years, or is it just me? Because sometimes it feels like it is just me and everyone else has opted to be a good mother.

When I went to the Grace to have Susan I took Simone de Beauvoir's *The Woman Destroyed*. *(Smiles.)*

My roommate's nightstand looked like Penny Leach's recommended reading list, or rather library, since she kept offering to lend me one. Her baby had piano fingers and feet already turned out in perfect little pliés.

You're interested in music, I said. *Did you study ballet?*

Her eyes glazed.

I paint. I want to paint full time now that the baby's come.

Oh, the baby won't be in my studio. I'll have my own space.

She turned away. "Mommy better check baby's diaper…"

My god, that was it. I had used the I word. I paint, I want, I'll have.

Everywhere I go, where there are children I see capable magnificent mothers nosing their children to the surface of music festivals, French immersion schools and dance lessons as steadily as a whale raises her baby to the surface to breathe oxygen.

ROSE takes off the pink heart.

Women who have put their own desires, goals, on hold. Women saving thoughts and ideas and actions until the kids are in bed, in playschool, school, university, gone.

Women who had teeny-tiny spotlights of their own. Exceptional women afraid to stop and ask, *What am I afraid of?*

You know there are stains on this dress, and they're not paint...they're blood.

Some of it's mine. This large-ish spot...

She points to her shoulder.

is from the day I was trying to get the baby asleep so I could read or have one intelligent thought unrelated to breastfeeding or resuming sexual relations. I was rocking so vigorously that the chair snapped a rocker and I flipped over onto the floor, striking my head on the coffee table. Oh yes the baby was safe, snoring into the exploded air bags, my breasts. I bled quite a bit that day. Well I certainly wasn't going to move and wake her up.

ROSE looks up dreamily.

There were some lovely patterns on the ceiling.

This blood...

ROSE points to her breast.

is from Bill's not-so-symbolic stump. And I'll tell you something, it doesn't matter if the breadwinner who has to leave the marriage bed in the morning is a car salesman, a stockbroker, or a university dean, the world takes its pound of flesh.

ROSE is speaking more to herself now. Deep in the moment, the symbol of their lives.

I do what I can for him. I press his wound to my heart until the bleeding has stopped. Because even with all the solitude that a remote control can inflict I see in his eyes that he is feeling as propped-up inside as I am. I've put this dress on for him too.

This stain…

Slowly her finger traces the boundaries of the stain on her lap.

well, we don't talk about this on Bliss Carmen Drive.

ROSE pauses deep in thought. She pulls herself up again.

My parents were dancers. They could waltz that great sweeping, turning waltz, 1, 2, 3… 1, 2, 3… 1, 2, 3…

ROSE waltzes…there is music in the background.

Other couples would leave the floor to watch them dance. My father says there are two tricks to waltzing.

ROSE stops as if giving instructions.

One, somebody has to lead—it doesn't have to be the man, it can be the woman, but one person leads and the other follows. Simple as that. And the other thing is, the woman has to step into the dance by putting her leg between the man's. She's got to be able to do that. She has got to take the partner and the dance on fully, because if she doesn't,

The music stops.

if she holds herself back, the beauty and the rhythm

of the waltz are unattainable.

ROSE smiles happily. This is a pleasant memory.

I remember the spring Bill and I fell in love. My god, the grass was never greener, the trees never more lush, and it never rained. I'd be standing in the grocery line up, or maybe at the bank, and suddenly our love-making the night before would come rushing back and I would look at the faces around me, astounded that they were unaware that the woman before them was clearly involved in some out-of-body sexual experience.

We wanted to know everything about each other and we played Twenty Questions long into the night. We asked, What are the names of all the people you've made love to? What attracted you to me? Are you a nurturing person? What are you afraid of?

Muslim men can divorce their wives by saying "I divorce you, I divorce you, I divorce you." Well, actually I'm not sure that it's Muslim men... I think it is. I knew once. Maybe it's Arabic men, but then Arabic is ethnic (?) and Muslim is a religion. The truth is I've lost great chunks of very important information and most of the time I can't disguise this fact.

Anyway, some males, some place, belonging to some religious and or ethnic group, can say I divorce you, I divorce you, I divorce you, like that three times, and that's it, the marriage is over. We have that here too.

There are things that, if we said them out loud, even once, the marriage would be over.

We wouldn't play Twenty Questions now.

The theme of the "Mary Tyler Moore Show" begins to play. ROSE moves happily to the music in an up beat mood as she prepares to start a painting. The voices of the household interrupt as she tries to manage getting them off for the day and paint.

You're off to work early. **Time to get up, Margaret, time to get up.** Tole painting. **Did you hear me, Margaret? Did you hear me?** *Don't ask me that now Susan I don't know when, OK.* Get the kids to their after-school activities. **I've poured your cereal. It's going to get soggy. Well then I don't care either.** *I care Susan but I have told you a million times looks aren't everything.* Oh scrub toilets and pick hair out of the sink, you want to join me? Well I hate the question. **Did you finish it? Did you finish it? Well I don't like repeating things a dozen times either.** You have asked me that every day since Susan was born. I don't have a plan, OK? *Susan, don't slam your books. Well it is a big deal, because I've told, I've asked you not to before.*

Are you doing your teeth? I said, well I'm not telling you what I said. Jesus if I made a plan, **YOUR TEETH** it would sure enough get completely screwed by 9:30. It's not PMS, CHRIST!

What time will you be home? That late? I didn't mean anything by it. No, I'm not accusing you, again. See you tonight…sometime.

Susan, you did it again. WHAT? You slammed your books. DON'T SLAM YOUR BOOKS did you get it that time? Well I'm sorry that you hate me but I'm still grounding you Friday night for slamming your fucking books.

ROSE's hand flies up to her mouth.

OOPS.

What I said Margaret was if you got up in the morning and did everything without being asked a thousand times, yes, yes I would drive you to school but you didn't so I won't. Good-bye. Have a good day.

ROSE calls after.

Love you!

Shit.

ROSE finally alone stands before the canvas. But is unable to begin.

Shit. Shit.

ROSE's voice cracks as she tries to gain control of her emotions. The MTM theme fades.

Bill might be, in a way, pleased to hear I've been to the library this morning. It's been a long time since I've been able to go into certain buildings at the university. The library, the SUB, oh and the Arts Centre. For over two months now I haven't even been able to walk across the campus.

The thing is at the university there is no avoiding EYOFUs, Eighteen-year-old female undergrads. EYOFUs.

I go prepared, I do, but every time I see an Eyofu sitting in the library or rushing down the hill to class I get this wrenching pain in my chest. It's not that they don't see me—they don't see me that's fine—it's that I see them. So I stopped going on campus. But I look at Susan and Margaret and I think I don't ever want to look at them and have this pain.

Susan has learned a new word. Icon. "I can't define it, but I know what it means." We are turning onto our street as she says this, and she shows off. Mr. Naugler's icon is his lawn. He is out on his postage stamp lawn applying Weed 'n Feed. We all grin and wave at him as we go by.

Bill says, "Very good Susan, what are our family's icons?"

"Margaret's is her Playstation, mine is the piano, and Dad's icon is," she pauses, "is your British Overlander."

"I don't think that's right," says Bill.

"Dad you never let us get drive-through in it..."

"What about Mom?" asks Bill. "What's her icon?"

"I don't know." Susan studies me. "The dog, I guess."

We all laugh.

"Well," I say, "Sheba loves me."

"I love you, Mommy," says Margaret.

"I love you, Mommy," says Susan.

We are all laughing, so Bill doesn't have to say anything.

The phone rings.

"Are you a nurturing person?" I said yes to that once. Turns out that should have been a big fat resounding No. With both babies, it was like I had entered this incredibly long dark tunnel.

A series of ten slides begin all are of the inside of a train tunnel slowly approaching the light at the end.

All through the pre-school years I struggled in that darkness. I don't know if they found any joy during that time, I don't remember giving any.

Finally the day came and Margaret started school. After a few months even my artist part emerged from the tunnel but with no body of work.

The intense white of the blank slide.

So far from where I thought I would be at 39. I was 39!

I didn't just get up this morning completely out of the blue and decide to wear my wedding dress to the IGA. There have been signs

> *ROSE takes the second grocery bag and removes her costume. A red silk shirt, a godawful pair of huge sweat pants, a large red Christmas wreath bow, a pair of men's glasses with a Victoria Secrets bra ad glued to the inside of one lens and a thong ad glued to the other.*

like February 14th, for instance, if Bill had been paying attention that day he would have seen this coming.

When I woke up last Valentine's Day I don't know what came over me. It was like a bolt of lightning: my mission to liberate all the forty-plus women on Bliss Carmen Drive from Valentine's Day.

> *ROSE begins to put the costume on over the wedding dress. The sweat pants hips are made huge when she tucks in the wedding dress.*

As soon as the house was empty I raced up the stairs and put on the sweat pants I scrub floors in and a red silk blouse. I spent a lot of time on my makeup, outlining my lips like they do now, only with black eyeliner, which was all I had.

> *Rose hurriedly puts on the makeup as described.*

I used a ton of blush on my cheeks and I tied a huge red bow in my hair. I took a pair of Bill's old glasses and glued a Victoria's Secret bra ad on one lens and a thong panty picture on the other. Black, of course.

A bra and then a thong ad are projected on to the screen.

On my chest I pinned a huge red heart that said Crazy Val's Bitter Valentine-O-Gram.

I walk to the first house and Jenny lets me in to her cherry-wood kitchen. I sit down in a chair and let the feelings wash over me, and I begin.

ROSE becomes the character CRAZY VAL who is over the top and has a definite edge.

CRAZY VAL: Valentine's Day—now there's a day fraught with disappointment. First of all it's the most romantic day of the year and I've got fifteen extra pounds of winter fat on me. I wasn't thinking, "Gee, it's Valentine's Day in six weeks" when I scarfed down that tenth shortbread cookie on New Year's Eve. So I'm not in top physical form, which is enough to make me bitter, but then there's the gift thing.

I think about his gift for a long time because I want it to show that I love him. And there is a gift from him of course there is, the lingerie.

ROSE whips a bra and thong out of her pocket.

Yes, the black push-up bra, and the thong. Oh God. So let's see, the hockey passes to the playoffs and the lingerie that makes something for him and something for…him.

But that's not the bitter part. The bitter part is that I have to put this stuff on…it's a gift. So I go into the bathroom and I start with the bra. OK, which is some other woman's size.

ROSE struggles to put it on over all the bulk.

Maybe the sales girl if she is a size 34A. But I figure out if I hold my breath all the way to the bed my nipples might just stay contained in the 1/8th of an inch of lace. As for the thong, the effect is completely lost in the three shortbread rolls that are around my hips. I open the bathroom door a few inches and I tell him to turn out the lights. I ask him, I beg him, please please don't make me come out with the lights on.

So halfway through the dash in the dark he turns on the light, and there is no place for me to hide. No place in the whole room where I can't see the light of lust die in his eyes. But the thing has been started and there's no turning back, and I know I've got thirty minutes of really hard work ahead of me.

But not this year.

I'm ready for tonight.

Things will be different tonight.

"Here Bill put your glasses on."

ROSE holds out BILL's glasses as though letting them slide up and down her body, a sad, wretched, revealed woman. ROSE returns.

ROSE: The women stand in their kitchens listening to CRAZY VAL's Bitter Valentine-O-Gram and they say:

"Who told you this?"

"Who sent you, Crazy Val?"

"How do you know this stuff?"

They speak some words before they are out of my mouth, they say:

fat
I love him.
lingerie
something for him
hold my breath
please please don't make me come out with the lights on
no place for me to hide

Slowly she takes off the bra and thong.

I think, by six o'clock tonight everyone in town and Bill will have heard about Crazy Val's Bitter Valentine-O-Gram. But he hasn't. No one has. It's like it never happened.

She removes the last of the makeup and the bow.

Well, my friend Lucy just returned from New York and it turns out Donna Robart's husband is doing my paintings. I don't know the painter's name. This is something Lucy and I started in Art History class. We always researched the names of the wives of the artists we were studying, maiden names if we could find them, and then in class we would refer to the artist as Lily Stumpf's hubby, or Mette Gad's other half, or Anne Bruegel's cutie, or Ida Nettleship's millstone.

Anyway, so what do six-foot paintings of people's insides go for? Fifteen to twenty-five thousand dollars according to Donna Robart's husband's gallery.

The day Lucy phoned to say, after three solo shows she had done *the painting*, she found her voice I wanted to congratulate her but I couldn't speak. I'd had galloping laryngitis for weeks.

The projector light comes on.

Sometimes on a bad day, like today, I have this fantasy that Greg Malone dressed as Barbara Frum, you know, the hair, the power shoulders, the works, suddenly appears, or rather just like on the old Journal is projected, onto my kitchen wall and there he is looking more like Barbara than even she did and he says to me:

A slide of Greg Malone, dressed as Barbara Frum looks out intently from the canvas.

"Are you bitter? Are you a bitter Rose, really bitter? Are you a bitter, bitter, Bitter Rose?"

And I stand up—my face now projected twenty-five, no a hundred times its normal size, and I say, *Yes, yes, yes I am bitter.*

I've never told any French Immersion mother this, but my first words to Margaret when the doctor handed her to me were "Are you going to let me paint the great Canadian Painting?"

Hello, my name is Bitter Rose I have two children and I want my own life.

Hello Bitter Rose, have we got a twelve-step cure for you.

I've refused to take the cure. But I haven't exactly painted the great Canadian painting either. That's what got me really down about Rhonda Brown. You see I am an avid walker too. It started when the kids were babies. I'd feed them supper and bath them and when Bill came in the door I would throw on my coat, say "supper's on the stove I'm going out for my walk." My walk. A chance to dream, to paint. Oh, the paintings I created on those walks. I could paint in an hour what it would take a mother with two young babies five years to paint. I didn't even try to put them down on canvas. It was enough to have them in my head. It saved me to have them in my head. But the thing is, if I were to die tomorrow and neighbours and friends were scrambling to come up with something to say about me, they might just say: *She was an avid walker.*

And then I got thinking about Rhonda Brown that maybe she wasn't out there walking off her supper but novels and short stories and poems and plays and paintings and symphonies and science and space and archaeology. Walking off all that stuff that got started in her head in Grade Seven.

Rhonda Brown, 46, daughter of, wife of, mother to...an avid walker, struck and killed while out walking.

> *Phone rings three times.*

> *ROSE begins to take out her tole painting supplies. She has a proper tole tote with all the paints brushes etc that she needs. She is working on a large country-style welcome sign. She talks as she sets up to tole paint.*

I get to stay in hotels quite a bit with Bill when he is consulting about Oceans and the Oh No Zone as Margaret calls it. Recently I was in the lobby of a hotel and a red-faced man came and sat in the armchair next to me. He was going out to celebrate. He had sold an investment and he had more money in his pocket that minute than he had made his entire working life and even though he was only a fireman, that's a lot of money.

> *ROSE will become the fire chief so she slips in and out of character.*

"You know that artist Maud Lewis?"

Yes.

"Do you have any of her paintings?"

No.

"Too bad, 'cause if you sold forty of them, like me, plus ten painted pots, six calendars, and two buckets, you would be waiting for a limo just like me."

I remarked that it was appalling the artist should live such an impoverished life and here he was celebrating off the spoils.

"Yeah," he said, "life is funny" and he told me this strange and remarkable tale.

ROSE stops painting and becomes JIM.

JIM: Maud and Everette Lewis lived on the edge of the Poor House Farm property. That was a big yellow residence where the poor folk and retarded ones—handicaps I guess they call them now, lived and farmed to pay their way. Anyways my grandmother's place was across right from them.

Old Everett often stopped in at Gram's to see if he could sell or barter something that Maud had painted. By the time Maud died, my grandmother had one of the largest collections of Maud Lewis paintings and memorabilia. There was an art dealer who made inquiries at that time, but he wasn't offering much money and Gram wasn't interested in selling.

When Gram died I cleared out her stuff for what I could get out of it. I tracked that art feller down and he offered a little more but I smelt that the market was heating up and I decided to bide my time.

Not too long after that we got a three bell alarm call out to the Poor Farm.

The sound of an alarm and trucks moving out.

It'd been empty since before Maud died and I always said some kid was going to arson the place and I was right. The smoke was mainly billowing out the back so we decided go in the front and figure out where to set the hoses. I don't know what gave me the presence of mind to do it but as soon as I seen that first one I turned to and sent everybody out. Smartest thing I ever did.

Guess you want to know what I saw, don't ya?

All around the room there was big canvases painted in Maud's primitive style, which was exciting, cause I knew in a controlled market situation, like if I didn't dump them all at once, there'd be a profit to be made. But then I saw that they was disgusting.

Well first off there was this 8' by 10' painting of a deformed baby being born, with a halo round its head like you see in olden day pictures. The mother, looking like the Virgin Mary, was a Down Syndrome for god's sake.

Then there was whole series of those poor farm retarded ones, naked and rolling in the strawberry fields. They was touching each other too, the women's nips were red strawberries, the men's wangs flowering vines. Well you can call it erotica but it was pornography to me.

But that was nothing compared to the last ones I saw. Little black kitties on skewers like kabobs, horses with bloody broken legs their sleighs tipped over, and the oxen had blood seeping out around their harnesses, pooling on to snow. Horrible disgusting pictures. But I only had to look at one or two to know they was Maud's, Maud bolder, perhaps, Maud more playful, but Maud all the same.

Outside the men were shouting, asking where to put the hoses. I told the boys to hold off, that there was poison inside, and I had to make a call to find out if it was harmful.

By the time I got to describing the ones of the kitty kabobs that art gallery owner was choking so hard he barely managed to get the words out but I read him loud and clear and I turned to the boys and I said LET HER BURN.

A slide of a fireman before a huge fire.

No I don't think it's a tremendous loss at all. People don't want paintings of kitten kabobs on aprons and tote bags. They want something cheerful. By burning those paintings I made Maud Lewis's place in history. Those other paintings, well, people would have wanted to bury her. As I told the gallery owner when he tried to beat me down on the buckets. If it wasn't for me, I said, you would have no business today, Maud Lewis is because of me.

ROSE is stunned by the story. She is looking at all the tole painting supplies laid out in front of her.

ROSE: I look at him. He's not real I decide. This red-faced destroyer of art, fire Chief, is a vision. I close my eyes. None of that happened, I tell myself. When I open my eyes he'll be gone. I leave them shut a long time. I think about the vision, what it might mean.

ROSE is struggling not to break down.

I think about all the tole painted buckets and calendars and pots I've done in four years. My head feels bound up and bursting at the same time. If I open my eyes and he's there it will be all true. If I open my eyes and he's not there I'll never pick up another tole paintbrush again.

ROSE looks at the empty chair and then tosses all her tole painting materials onto the floor. ROSE begins to organize her artist paints.

When we were first together Bill said to me...when he still believed I was going to do the artist thing...

"Promise me," he said. "Promise me I won't ever walk into a gallery and see my face on the wall. Don't ever use me as a subject for your paintings."

I said, but I was planning a series of lithographs: *Man in Torn Shorts Wanting Sex.* Oh well, I said, they would never sell. Most every woman has one in her bedroom already she wouldn't want to have one in her living room too.

The secret to never being compromised, my mother told me when I was about that age and she was desperate to keep me safe, is to never find yourself in a compromising position.

She never explained to me what exactly a compromising position was. She never warned me that it would be in bed with my husband, with my children dreaming in the rooms down the hall in a very cheery house, on a very desirable street, in a liberal arts town without my own money.

I look at some couples—well, many couples actually—and I think, didn't they see that they were going to make each other miserable every day of their lives? How in hell did they ever get together? Of course the short answer is sex and the long answer is sex too.

They say a half-dog, half-wolf pet is never trustworthy. For years it may be fine, make a fool of itself when its belly is scratched, let the baby pull its ears, sleep in the curve of the toddler's back at night. The parents start thinking it's as safe as a big dumb Lab. Then one day, totally unprovoked, like lightning it streaks across the living-room carpet and attacks the toddler. It was the way the child moved at that moment. Somewhere in the animal's brain, that motion, that shape, said PREY—ATTACK NOW, and the wolf-dog, blocking out the rational, the relationship with the family, and the love it had for the child, attacks. Tragic and predictable.

There is no romance. Love is just a romantic idea we have invented to make life more interesting or agonizing, depending on how you decide to look at it. Flowers, candy, candlelight, all fiction. The truth is, the person you happened to be with, or dating maybe, or saw across a crowded room, moved in a certain way, imprinted a shape on your brain and the sexual instinct said NOW. It didn't say, is this person an idiot? Is this person's taste in videos the last run of shad? Is this person's compulsive sports watching, channel flicking, lack of basic map skills, going to be a problem down the road? No! None of it! Movement = shape = sex.

Of course, sixteen years later, it's a pretty bloody scene for everyone. But applying rational thought to the scene is just as ludicrous as thinking a wolf dog is as trustworthy as a big dumb Lab.

The heart that symbolizes romance in our society is a powerful symbol.

ROSE brings out an easel and turns it.

This is an imprint of my painted bum.

ROSE takes out a black marker and draws a heart around the outline. Inside she writes Bill loves Rose.

Knowing this is freeing I think. I say to myself, it's not my fault, it's not Bill's fault. It's a case of misshapen identity.

When all this began, this metaphoric thing, I bought a bikini. I wear it strictly for the tan lines, which I find funny and sexy at the same time. I stand in the mirror and grin at my body all my exciting bits exposed in gleaming white.

When I was a girl of ten I skinned rabbits. Every second day in winter I would follow my brother into the woods to check our snares. Often there were the stiff frozen corpses, laid out as though still in the act of running. Once in my snare, we found one newly caught. I cried until my brother killed it with his own hands because the noose was already too tightly drawn and I didn't want to leave it. For once knowing exactly the suffering I inflicted.

Later in the sour cellar, the rabbit hung by its back legs, I cut precisely so as not to damage the coat. I peeled back its skin inch by inch, exposing its blue flesh, veined in purple, gleaming maps to the terrible vulnerability of its soft body.

ROSE pauses hugging her own body.

I recently read the saddest story in the world. No, not the saddest, the most harrowing. After I read it I went to bed and cried. I had to go to bed even though it was arsenic hour, even though I had fifteen minutes to get supper on the table and twenty-nine minutes to get Margaret to Brownies and Susan to piano.

An artist, a man of great talent and influence, described how one night at a launching of a book of his work he noticed "a middle-aged woman watching him from a little distance away and even though several times there clearly was an opening for her to come forward and have her copy signed, she did not." Finally when the room was almost cleared and even he had begun to get ready to leave, "she propelled herself forward as if toward her own death."

"Excuse me," she said, "I want to ask you, when you are an artist and you don't have any work... what I mean is you haven't created a body of work yet, how do you call yourself an artist?"

Oh my god.

The great artist gave a very kind and helpful answer…but for days I've been caught prisoner in that place where she is just about to be propelled forward.

Did he have to say middle-aged? Did he have to write, "as if propelled towards her own death?" Did he have to write down those words, "How do you call yourself an artist without a body of work?" Did he have to peel back my skin inch by inch by inch?

The projector is fired up again.

I had a dream last night. It's opening night of my own solo show in the big TO. Everyone I ever told I was going to be a painter is there, including the Penny Leach mother from hell, and there are several skinless rabbits feasting on the reception food. But as soon as I drift in, magnificently, I see there is a problem.

The slides begin to click through. Each is blank accept for a large, scrawling" ROSE" at the bottom.

All the canvases on the wall, signed with great flourish, are blank. People are shocked—and I am shocked. I knew I hadn't done any paintings, but I was expecting startling, innovative work.

There is no applause as I enter the room. There are smirks and whispers and I told you so looks. Clearly there is some need for an explanation. I step forward and I say: "These canvases are blank because I am a head-based artist."

Even though as soon as I had seen the blank canvases I had started telling myself this is a dream, Rose, this is just a dream I can't prevent what happens next which is that the Penny Leach

mother steps forward wrenches open the top of my
head and announces: "Well, there may have been
something here once but it has atrophied like her
children."

Gerta gets edgy with us sometimes. Well, pissed off.
I know she listens to us talking and our bitterness
pisses her off. We have everything and of course
we do. She says to us, "Four years is too long to be
in Tole Painting Level One!" We tell her we want to
move on as a group, but the weeping playwright
who cries in her paint is not ready for Level Two.
We've also made a secret pact that no one will drop
out because Gerta would naturally fill it with a new
beginner and things would never be the same. And
we need them to be the same here because there is
something in motion, moving away from us, out in
the world.

I've lost a lot of weight. Twenty pounds in one
month. Every bit of food I put into my mouth is
cardboard. My friends rave. "You look great, how
did you do it? If you've been sick I insist you breathe
on me this minute. I don't care if it's fatal, at least
I'll be thin in the casket." I think that they are just
saying this. I think they must see the hollowness
in my eyes, hear the desperation in my throat. But
other friends call, "You look fabulous, I hear. Come
on, tell us your secret!" At last I say, "Betrayal. I've
lost twenty pounds because of a betrayal."

They assume it's Bill, of course. "Wouldn't you
know it," they laugh. "Betrayal makes me eat. The
last time I was betrayed I gained 37 lbs."

This morning, at breakfast, Bill, referring to his
graduate student of three months, he said, "She is
spirited and intelligent." How long has it been since
I felt spirited and intelligent?

This is the graduate student who read his paper

"Our Bodies, Beluga Bodies" on the net and flew across the country to study with him.

She is researching his new book. He is taking her out to dinner because she is putting in long hours at the library. He is telling me because he is not hiding anything and that's just what he didn't want me to think that this is some sort of—-my word— betrayal.

After he leaves I am seized by distress and I am distressed by it. I never wanted to see spirited, intelligent women as threats. I never wanted this relationship to be everything. I never planned for it to be my icon.

The phone rings.

Anyway it isn't Bill's betrayal.

The deep betrayal, the one that the women at tole painting can't bear to think about, is the betrayal of that twelve-year-old girl still there inside of them, inside of me.

I sat in the kitchen this morning after he had gone to meet the graduate student and I thought and I thought and I thought, *What are you afraid of, Rose?*

I'm one of those people who pull back. If I was on one of those 911 TV shows, reality based shows, I would be the one on the bank of the raging river screaming *Someone has got to save that child!* Just at the point when the most is required of me I hold back.

The year Margaret turned seven and Susan, ten, I started to paint again. I completed ten miniatures and the first painting of a series on women in their state of the art kitchens. Lucy was very excited about the project. I sent her *The Coffee Party* slide. Four women bathed in mid-morning light sit at a breakfast nook, a half-eaten cheesecake in the centre of the table. They causally talk seemingly unaware that the hostess has her wrists bound, her hands purple with rage and her mouth taped shut, lips crudely drawn on with lipstick. No one is moving to take the cake knife from her that she holds to her throat perhaps to cut the tape, perhaps to slash her jugular. All the women have their own scars rising out of their own collars.

Lucy phoned me expensive time and said, "It's going to be a wonderful show, Rose, I feel it." She took the slide to her gallery and of course the owner couldn't commit but if the project was as good as it sounded and the paintings as interesting as the first, Lucy was sure he would seriously consider a show in his second space.

Toronto, God. Nothing like a minuscule chance of my own show, in a not-very-well-known gallery's second space but in Toronto to restore the balance of power in my head. God, I was so horny. I hate that word, but that's what I was.

The next morning, after everyone had gone, I pressed my face to the bathroom mirror and I cried. *I am pregnant. I am pregnant.*

It's only been nine hours, but I know that I am. I can't enter that long dark tunnel again.

> *ROSE paints her hand with black paint.*

Bill says, "First have the test done, and then you decide."

But I know that I am. And I am. I am caught as fast as that struggling rabbit in the snare. And what has to be done has to be done by my hand.

> *ROSE imprints her black hand print on the stain in her lap.*

I can't enter that dark place again.

After everything.

I start painting again. But the paintings are terrible. They don't work. They are the same ones I planned, but I'm not the same person.

What I want to paint are the faces of those women. The giggly fourteen-year-old woman and her tight-mouthed determined mother. The second-trimester woman weeping and the tenderness in the face of the old Lebanese grandmother who stroked and kissed her cheek. No, what I want most to paint is the tip of the nozzle that entered me.

I want to paint my legs and feet splayed as if in giving birth.

Oh God.

I want to paint the deep, stainless, stain less steel sink, and the exact colour of what was washed away in it.

I want to put my face in a painting.

A painting of a woman alone on the edge of a bank long after the water is still.

I'm starting those paintings today.

ROSE unzips the wedding dress letting it fall away. She steps out of it leaving it in a heap on the floor.

Making these paintings won't change…what I mean to say is that they won't bring that child back.

ROSE begins to say that she is sorry. Note: I've put the names of people in brackets to help the actor direct the emotion.

I'm sorry (her children)

I'm sorry (to Bill)

I am sorry (to the child)

But I promise you that I will enter that water and dive as deeply as I have to, for as long as it takes even if my lungs burst with the want of air until I reach your body and bring you to the surface. If it takes all my strength I'll bring you onto the bank and I'll say, *I did this. I did not save this child, because I was afraid of drowning myself.*

I will not be bitter. I will not be a bitter Rose.

I won't hold myself back.

I will take my art on and where it leads me, I will go, and the rhythm and the beauty will be there. 1, 2, 3... 1, 2, 3...

    ROSE moves to the canvas and begins to paint.

    The End.

THREE STOREY, OCEAN VIEW

This play is dedicated to Jane Laura McLauchlan,
with love and gratitude.

Acknowledgements

The playwright wishes to thank and ackowledge the care and attention this play received over the years it took to finish it from the following wonderful artists and friends: Tessa Mendel, Philip Adams, Pamela Halstead, Marina Endicott, Kim McCaw, Yvette Nolan, Paula Danckert, Mary Vingoe, Laura McLauchlan, Leah Hamilton, Claudia Mitchell, Ann Marie Kerr, and Colleen Murphy.

Three Storey, Ocean View was developed with the assistance of The Canada Council for the Arts, the Nova Scotia Arts Council, the Banff Playwright's Colony, Playwrights Atlantic Resource Centre, Mulgrave Road Theatre, and Equity Showcase Toronto.

Production History

Three Storey, Ocean View premiered at Mulgrave Road Theatre, Guysborough, NS, in October, 2000, with the following cast:

RUTH.. Marguerite McNeil

PEG.. Mary-Colin Chisholm

ZOE ....Kelly O'Neill

ENID .... Mauralea Austin

BONNIE.. Cindy O'Neill

CINDY .... Nicole Moore

SHERI.. Genevieve Steele

DAVID .... Michael Pellerin

BEULAH.. Bev Brett

CAROL .... Carol Godsman

LUD.. Bill Forbes

MARSHA.. Keirsten Tough

Directed by Philip Adams

Dramaturged by Yvette Nolan

Set design by Denyse Karn

Sound design by Paul Cram

Costume design by Denise Barrett

Light design by Lee Riggs

Stage Manager: Georgina Brown

The very important second production by Equity Showcase Toronto took place in 2003 directed (and dramaturged) by Pamela Halstead.

Setting and Characters

Late 1990s, late May, mid-afternoon to 2:30 am

PEG-45-so weary but still trying
RUTH-61-Peg's mother, suffers from dementia
ZOË -14-Peg's daughter, determinedly out of control

1960s, November, early morning to noon

BONNIE-39-obese
CINDY-13- Bonnie's daughter, black heritage, self-conscious
TOMMY 12- offstage only. Mouthy.

1970s, summer, July, midnight to mid-morning

SHERI-23- the bride
DAVID-35-Acadian, the groom
BEULAH-45-Sheri's former mother-in-law

1980s, February, noon to late afternoon

LUD-53-stroke victim
CAROL-50-Lud's wife of 32 years
MARSHA-17-drop-out, home from the city

ENID-61-Ruth's childhood friend, she has lived next to this house all her life and appears in all of the stories. In the 60s, she is 38. In the 70s, 45. In the 80s, she is 53.

Act I

Scene One

There are five spaces: kitchen with a sun-porch alcove, downstairs bedroom, upstairs bedroom, widow's walk and deck of a boat. There is some furniture left behind in the house, table, chair, and two beds. The widow's walk is filled with bottles left over from drinking parties.

ZOË enters the central space from within the house. She is fussing with a tear in the seat of her pants. PEG bangs loudly on the door from the outside.

PEG: *(Offstage.)* Zoë? Zooooeee.

ZOË looks around very unimpressed with what she sees.

(O.S.) Unlock the door.

ZOË pushes open the bedroom door and looks in.

ZOË: Gross.

PEG: *(O.S.)* We are not going back to Toronto until I have looked at this house.

ZOË walks over and unlocks the door. PEG enters.

Must everything be a fight?

ZOË silently displays the tear in her jeans.

Isn't the shredded look in? For god sakes they're only jeans. It isn't my fault that the agent isn't here

with a key. I came all this way to see this house and
I am going to see this house.

ZOË sits on the floor.

(Trying.) It doesn't look so bad on the inside. There
is wonderful light in here. Look—bay windows
looking out onto the bay—thus the name! I bet
under this crappy linoleum is a beautiful hardwood
floor. Or pine.

Did you see the barn? It's a perfect place for a kiln. I
can be as messy as I want out there. A real studio. A
view of the ocean. A lovely little village filled with
(Small grin.) villagers. It has everything, everything
we want, doesn't it? Come on, Zoë, admit it this
place has amazing potential.

ZOË continues to ignore her.

You're here now—will it kill you to look around?

ZOË walks out of the house. PEG calls after her.

Bring Gram in.

(To herself.) Long term relationship.

The bigger picture. Good Christ. I would have to be
Christ.

*PEG takes a slow turn around the room. Looks in the
small bedroom then returns centre stage to gaze out
at the ocean. ZOË enters.*

PEG: Where's Gram? You know Zoë this is like getting so
           old.

RUTH: *(O.S.)* Peg. PEG. *(Rising panic.)* PEG.

           PEG goes out.

PEG: *(O.S.)* Mom this way! Rule #1. Never go down to
           the beach without me.

RUTH: (O.S.) I don't want you to catch this.

             PEG brings RUTH to the threshold.

PEG: I won't. I've told you a thousand times I can't.

RUTH: No. NO.

PEG: Come on, come in.

RUTH: Not my house.

PEG: It's the house we have come to see by the sea.
             Remember? The one for sale. Close your eyes. Close
             them. OK, Zoë and I have a surprise.

                   *PEG gently pulls RUTH into the room. RUTH is
                   carrying a hard covered sketch book, which is very
                   old and falling apart. As RUTH enters the house the
                   other spaces in the house light up. BONNIE rolls
                   over in the bed, SHERI (Dressed in her wedding
                   mini-dress.) removes her veil, and CAROL fills a
                   pipe. RUTH stops.*

RUTH: (Pulling back.) Peg whose house is this.

PEG: The house is empty Mom— Ahhh keep your eyes
             closed. It's the one for sale.

             The lights go down in the other spaces.

             It's the one in the village where you grew up. The
             house we have come home to look at. Watch it
             there. OK.

ZOË: (Sighs.)

PEG: Zoë—that chair. Don't peek. Now sit. There. OK!
             Open your eyes!

             RUTH sits looking out at the water.

RUTH: Oh dear. Dear. Water not enough no water not no.

PEG: Don't get upset, of course there's enough water it's the ocean. It must be low tide. This coast has the lowest tides in the world. Remember Zoë you learned that in what, grade six?

            RUTH is flipping pages in her sketchbook, she finds the one she is looking for.

RUTH: No. *(Pause.)* No rocks… *(Shakes her head.)* Not my beach.

PEG: It's the same beach Mom. Dad's sketch is from another angle that's all.

RUTH: Oh no, gone. Water gone. NO good. No good. Go home Home home.

PEG: We are home. We have travelled 2000 kilometres to get you home. This is the village where you grew up. This is HOME.

RUTH: Dear dear. No no no good for it. It.

            ZOË groans.

PEG: It is good for it. Whatever it is, it is good for it. We are here for a whole month.

ZOË: What? You said… *(Realizing.)*

PEG: Gram thought the cat had got your tongue.

RUTH: Cat got your tongue!

ZOË: Don't say that.

RUTH: Cat got your tongue!

ZOË: Gram, don't say that.

RUTH: *(Behind her hand.)* Cat got your tongue.

PEG: Mom. Mom, Mom. Shhh. Do you have another picture of the beach?

RUTH starts poring over her sketch book.

ZOË: She gets sick so my life gets ruined.

PEG: Zoë, she hear things, she understands things.

ZOË: I'm missing school.

PEG: What, you've forgotten that you're suspended?

BONNIE rolls over in the bed.

BONNIE: *(Mumbles.)* Pappy? Pappy?

RUTH: Whose house is this?

PEG: *(Snapping.)* It's the one for sale.

ZOË: When are we going?

PEG: After the real estate agent gets here and we see the house.

ZOË: I see it —it's a dump. I'm cold.

RUTH: It is a different kind of cold.

PEG: It is a beautiful May afternoon it isn't cold.

ZOË: *(Deliberate.)* I'm sooooo hungry.

RUTH: Oh hungry, Oh Henry.

PEG: Zoë!

RUTH: Oh hungry—Oh Henry.

PEG: Don't start that. We had hours of that in the car.

RUTH: Oh hungry—Oh Henry.

PEG: We just ate. You had a good lunch.

RUTH: You had a good breakfast. Oh Hungry.

PEG: You had a good lunch. You had the lobster roll, remember?

RUTH: Oh Oh hungry oh…

                ZOË gives RUTH an Oh Henry bar. PEG looks at ZOË.

ZOË: I bought it. At the garage. I bought it.

PEG: I believe you.

ZOË: "'Cause that's our rule."

PEG: I am going to look around. Look, a downstairs bedroom. Perfect for Gram.

                ZOË follows her into the bedroom.

ZOË: I am not living here. I'm not.

PEG: OK. Live with your father then.

ZOË: I can't, that bitch—

PEG: No, not OK.

ZOË: That person is there all the time with her PERFECT pink daughter.

PEG: You have to learn to get along.

ZOË: No.

PEG: Grow up. You are almost fifteen. You don't even see what people are doing for you—giving up for you.

ZOË: No one's giving up anything for me. You're giving up school so YOU can afford a house. I don't want a house—you want a *(Under her breath.)* dump.

PEG: OK, let's live on the streets. Fun.

ZOË   I can live with my friends.

                They walk into LUD's space.

PEG: Oh yes—your *(so called)* friends.

ZOË:	You don't know them. You were never around.
PEG:	I was busy but I was around.
ZOË:	Unless you had someone better to do ooops something better to do.
PEG	It's not as if you were ever home. Lots of times I was home but you were...where exactly?
ZOË:	You went to art school so you could divorce Daddy.
PEG:	No that wasn't the plan it simply happened.
ZOË:	"God Peg I feel so violated."

PEG looks taken aback.

(Small laugh.) I love that line. I know everything.

PEG:	No, you don't know everything. *(Trying.)* I know it's been a tough year for everyone.
ZOË:	YOU were happy.
PEG:	It wasn't a lark for me.
ZOË:	Happy happy happy happy.
PEG:	Well you showed us you weren't happy. So Mommy has to come back home and everything has to be the way it was for Zoë.
ZOË:	It isn't.
PEG:	No. I've got a mother to care for, a daughter to bring up and no home.
ZOË:	Whose fault is that?
PEG:	You don't have to be excited but could you give this little plan a chance?
ZOË:	You're wasting the settlement money.

PEG: Geronimo. Hear the word and leave it there.

ZOË: Phoney therapist phoney word.

PEG: OK if you don't want to use the tools fine, but I am not discussing with you what I am doing with my settlement.

ZOË: That's not fair. I'm affected I should have a say.

PEG: Responsible people get to vote.

ZOË: So everything is all your fault but you still get to make all the decisions.

PEG: Right, it was me who tubed vodka down your throat.

ZOË: Tubed?

PEG: Whatever you call it when some party animal shoves a tube down your throat and pours vodka into your stomach. Alcohol poisoning—you could have died.

ZOË: So I am grounded from My Entire Life FOREVER. That's responsible parenting.

PEG: Coming here is not about me being Mean Mom.

ZOË: No it's about you hating me.

PEG: Sometimes Zoë you say the most…(hurtful things.) Truce OK? I hate this fighting…where are you going?

> *ZOË leaves the room. PEG stands for a minute then follows her into the kitchen just as ZOË leaves the house.*

(*Softly.*) Zoë.

> *The other rooms light up 1,2,3 times like a pulse revealing the lives in the other room RUTH picks up*

on the energy and looks around listening carefully.
She goes to a door and hides behind it.

Well the family trip is working, we're feeling closer
all ready.

She watches RUTH peeking around the door.

What's up?

RUTH: *(Whispering.)* What are the names of the people in
this house?

PEG: Peg and Ruth. Ruth and Peg. Come and sit down.
Are you happy to be in your little home village with
(Counting.) 1, 2, 3 steeples! Did you go to church
when you were little? Well we'll start. I'll put Zoë
in Sunday School. That will shake God up eh?

RUTH: Not my one one. This this.

PEG: No. We went by the home place. There were flower
beds. The home place isn't for sale but this one is.
Should we buy it?

RUTH: Where's my money in the book one?

PEG gets it for her. RUTH grabs it delighted.

PEG: Money bags. Don't lose it we need every cent.

RUTH: Help Peg.

PEG: OK let's see if this place is worth all our money put
together. Can you manage the stairway?

RUTH: No not my house Peg.

PEG Mom! Please please try.

RUTH: *(Banging her head.)* Stupid one head. Stupid awful
one.

PEG: It's OK.

> *Takes RUTH's face in her hands.*

RUTH   No you catch this this no no.

PEG: Shhh look at the pretty water. You could wake up
              to that everyday eh?

> *PEG goes up the stairs.*

RUTH: Not the water.

> *She stands passing her hand over her head.*

Scene Two

> *Lights up in BONNIE's space where she is sleeping.*

CINDY: (O.S.) Get up Tommy. It's 7:30.

TOMMY: (O.S.) I got cramps.

> *BONNIE stirs in her bed.*

CINDY: (O.S.) Shh…don't wake her up.

TOMMY: (O.S.) I said I got cramps.

BONNIE: (Warning groan.)

CINDY: (O.S.) You got a test today?

BONNIE: Cindy!

CINDY: (O.S.) Shhhh…

> *All is quiet.*

BONNIE: CINDY.

> *CINDY comes down the stairs and into BONNIE's
> room.*

CINDY: What?

BONNIE: What's going on up there?

CINDY:	He won't get up.
BONNIE:	*(Bellows.)* Tommy! You get up for your sister.

CINDY goes back upstairs.

TOMMY:	*(O.S.)* I said I got cramps.
CINDY:	*(O.S.)* He says he's got cramps.
BONNIE:	He'll have more than cramps if I have to come up there. Do you want me to get Cindy to send your father home after you?

Silence.

Is he getting up?

CINDY:	*(O.S.)* Yessss…ouch!
BONNIE:	You leave her alone and get your arse downstairs. Cindy?
CINDY:	*(O.S.)* Yes.
BONNIE:	Bring me my purse I need bread for lunches.

Scene Three

Upstairs bedroom. SHERI is wearing a white wedding dress (Mini). She struggles with the zipper while DAVID stares out the window.

SHERI:	David help me.

DAVID hands her an envelope.

What's this?

DAVID:	From Mom and Dad.

SHERI reads the card.

SHERI:	What did you say?

DAVID: Merci.

SHERI: It's close to the water there.

DAVID: Sure it's on the point but the tide never comes up that far.

            DAVID slips the dress over her head—she stands in a white slip edged in lace.

SHERI: I thought we might get a lot in on the lake road.

DAVID: Them giving us the land means we can build more house. We can start it this fall.

            DAVID rubs her belly.

            She's sleeping.

SHERI: What if she is a he?

DAVID: Ta mere ne sait pas ca que je sait.

SHERI: What? What did you say?

DAVID: I said, You don't know about these things.

SHERI: I guess I know more than you. Don't forget...

DAVID: ...Garyleigh. I'm not. But I know what I know *(Whispers.)* eh Magi?

SHERI: That isn't even a real name.

DAVID: Neither was Sheri once.

            DAVID drifts back to the window.

            "The Journey of the Magi" was the most beautiful poem I studied at school so I named my boat *The Journey* and I name our daughter Magi.

SHERI: If we were to build out there I won't want no windows facing the water.

DAVID:	No windows on three sides of the house?
SHERI:	'Cause when you weren't on the water you would be watching it like you are doin' right now.
DAVID:	It isn't a woman…you don't have to be jealous.
SHERI:	Ha, a woman'd be easy to fix.
DAVID:	And what would you do to fix her?
SHERI:	I ain't telling you 'cause you might think you're worth it.
DAVID:	Yeah?

He moves in on her.

| SHERI: | Hey! You said you wanted to leave the dance 'cause you was tired. |
| DAVID: | That's what I said. |

Scene Four

CAROL is helping LUD to his large wooden chair next to a table. His left side is paralyzed and he has limited movement on his right side. He leans heavily on CAROL as he walks, using a cane on his good side.

CAROL: There, get your pins under you first. You're OK. I'm not going to let you fall. I could but I won't eh?

LUD settles into the chair.

There. Now. You won't have to go pee when Marsha is here. You hear me? You've done your business so don't ask her to take you.

LUD: p-p-p-p-

CAROL: What?

LUD: p-p-p—ipe

CAROL: Oh you want your pipe do you? You can have it.

LUD: *(Disgruntled.)* ppppp- (louder) ppppp—-ipe.

CAROL: I filled it for you. I'm not going to give it to you too.

> *LUD struggles to get the pipe from the ashtray. He puts it in his mouth and waits. CAROL glances over at him but continues to get ready to go.*

Got that lit yet?

LUD: NNNNooooo.

CAROL: You done it before you can do it again. The doctor told you, you have to do what you can for yourself.

> *LUD struggles to get the box of matches. He drops it on the floor.*

Now what are you going to do?

> *He kicks it across the room.*

Now you've done it. Have to get it when I get home from town I guess.

> *LUD stamps his feet. Stamp Stamp Stamp.*

Don't start that. Stop it.

> *She waits until he stops.*

I'll only be gone one hour.

> *LUD Stamp Stamp Stamp.*

One. You'll survive. Marsha's coming over, you liked Marsha.

> *He stops his feet.*

Yes toddling out to the barn with Lud to feed the cows.

She retrieves the box of matches giving it to him.

You know if I light it, I smoke it.

LUD grins and gives a slow halting laugh.

Scene Five

RUTH sits alone in the kitchen.

ENID: (O.S.) Hello. Hellloo.

RUTH: Hello. Hellloo.

ENID enters.

ENID: I'm from across the way—the agent's coming out is he? Oh my dear. As I live and /

RUTH: / breathe.

ENID: Ruth Alice Atwood? I saw they was Ontario plates but I never thought I would walk and here and see you!

RUTH: *(Urgently.)* Water. There water gone. Gone oh dear.

ENID: You know me? Ruthie you know me? I am an old woman I've put on a few pounds but I am still Enid.

She looks closely at RUTH who hardly glances at her.

RUTH: Not enough water no no no.

ENID: *(Slowly.)* Well it's low tide. *(Allowing herself to know.)* Oh my dear Ruthie.

RUTH: Oh my dear. Gone all gone. Not not enough.

She passes her hand over her head.

ENID: The tide is only gone out. The water is out there. The water will come back. *(Softly.)* Well, you're the

| | image of your mother. Don't suppose you want to hear that though. |
| RUTH: | The water will be back. Good. Good. |

RUTH begins to look through her sketch book.

ENID:	Oh my landy is that your old sketch book from all those years ago. *(Laughs.)* I haven't said Oh my landy since Christ wore sneakers to the prom.
RUTH:	Beach…rocks no rocks no tsk tsk tsk.
ENID:	No it's not the same beach is it?
RUTH:	Not the same beach. *(Nods.)* Not the one one.
ENID:	All those rocks came in years ago. You still have that one of me in my bathing suit, do you?

RUTH concentrates as she looks through the pages.

| RUTH: | Enid. *(Points.)* Enid. |
| ENID: | Oh my. All these years you kept that thing. I don't look like that in a bathing suit now. Jack wanted that picture but, no, you wouldn't give it to him. You remember Jack? |

RUTH looks through the pages.

You never did one of Jack, you didn't like Jack very much. Oh there's Frankie.

| RUTH: | Shhhshhhs. |

RUTH takes the sketches away from ENID.

ENID:	Why dear?
RUTH:	Don't don't shhh it shh shh don't.
ENID:	All right dear. All right. I heard you had a daughter she must be upstairs is she?

RUTH: Peg.

ENID: I never had kids…cats was all we had. So your Peg, she's thinking to buy this place?

RUTH: *(Takes out the bank book.)* Money book. Help Peg.

ENID: Want to help her out do you? Well some have to don't they? Did you go by the home place?

             RUTH is fussing with the money book until she gets it out of sight.

             You wouldn't want the home place now. Americans bought it, ripped the siding off, shingled it, left it bare. No paint she said because they wanted to restore it to its original condition. I told her when that house was built people painted their houses. Exposed beams insides, your mother would have a fit. The yard looks good though. They carted away your father's old cars. The yard looks good. You never came home for their funerals.

             CINDY enters from the stairs. She is intent on trying to get the zipper of her jacket, which is shabby and too small, done up.

BONNIE: That you Cindy?

             RUTH is startled.

RUTH: Who are the ones in this house?

ENID: People you mean? Well Ruth, Enid. Peg is upstair. I thought I saw a youngster too—is there a girl with you.

RUTH: Yes there.

             RUTH follows CINDY into the bedroom. ENID looks in too.

ENID: Nobody is here.

RUTH looks from CINDY to BONNIE to ENID.

I use to think about you an awful lot. You made out all right in Ontario did you? You had a good life there, did you Ruthie?

CINDY: Mom I got your purse.

BONNIE: Just once I would like to wake up to a pleasant day without a goddamn row bringing the house down around my ears. I am telling his father this time. *(Shouts to the ceiling.)* I'm telling him mister!

ENID: I couldn't have moved up there can't imagine living in a place where you don't know your neighbours from Adam.

BONNIE: I was having a good dream too, about my Pappy. You go tell him he's going to have to be happy with Puffs because there ain't no bread or eggs.

CINDY: He knows—he don't want no Puffs.

ENID: Lots of the young ones now have to leave now that the fishing is finished. None of us ever dreamed the fish would stop.

BONNIE: Some dreams seem realer than others don't they.

CINDY: Mom the teacher said if I am late again I have to go to the principal's office.

BONNIE: Oh she did, did she? Did you ask her why she is growing a beard?

CINDY: Moooommm.

BONNIE: TOMMMMMMMYYYY.

RUTH comes out of the bedroom and goes to the stairs looking up.

ENID: You want Peg? Want me to call her down?

RUTH:	Whose house one one?
ENID:	Oh it belongs to the family of that American artist woman who owned when we was girls. She died so they're selling it. She stopped coming in the sixties. Got Jack to caretake it for years renting it out to this one and that one enough to keep the repairs up.
BONNIE:	You go tell him I want that wood box filled to the brim before he steps out of this house.
ENID:	You remember Billy Hamilton the coloured fellar don't you? Well he married the youngest Bruce girl Bonnie and they lived here. Bonnie got so fat and lazy she could hardly make it out of bed.

ENID continues to talk but RUTH is listening to the voices around her.

BONNIE:	Go on. Go tell him.
CINDY:	He don't listen to me.
BONNIE:	He better listen.

CINDY goes up the stairs.

CINDY:	(O.S.) Mom wants you to fill the wood box (Beat.) please.
TOMMY:	(O.S.) No frigging way.
BONNIE:	What did he say? What did he say?
CINDY:	(O.S.) He said. He said no frigging way.
BONNIE:	He said that? He said that? By the liftin' do I have to come after you mister man?

TOMMY stomps down the stairs and out the front door.

ENID:	After them little Sheri Bishop lived here with her husband, Buddy. He was lost over the side. David,

Frenchy's son, moved in with her pretty soon after, too soon some (I) thought.

BONNIE: Your father is going to hear about this. You hear me? Using the F word.

BONNIE enters the kitchen.

CINDY: He went out the front.

BONNIE: Where does he go so early? The both of yahs? Wait till I tell Bill. Old Tom's gonna get his arse tanned see if he don't.

CINDY: Mom you want me to go to the corner?

BONNIE: Get my purse.

ENID: The last ones to rent the place was Lud and Carol from in back of the lake. Lived here after his stroke after they lost their farm. Lud drowned out there in the ditch.

RUTH looks out the window intently.

You looking for the ditch? It's gone. Neighbours came and filled it in after so Carol wouldn't have to look out on to it. That woman was nothing but a saint for years.

CINDY hands BONNIE the purse.

RUTH: Where's my purse?

ENID: Lost it have you?

BONNIE: I'd go after him if it weren't for my legs. I step outside, it don't bother me none but then in the night the pains shoot up from my feet something' awful.

The lights come up in the upper bedroom as DAVID and SHERI lay holding each other. RUTH is pulled up the stairs and into their room.

ENID: Like her mother went...gone just like she did in the end.

                 ENID tries a light but it doesn't work. She disappears out the door.

Scene Six

BONNIE: That jacket's gettin' small? Zipper's gaping is it? Why don't you sew it?

CINDY: We don't have a needle.

BONNIE: Get your father to get one from the Home Ec. Room. She won't miss it.

CINDY: Mmooom.

BONNIE: If she does old Bill will remind her of a thing or two.

CINDY: Mom I'll be late.

BONNIE: You got a whole hour. There before the teachers even. What do you do?

CINDY: I've been late two times this week. If I am late again I'll have to go to the/

BONNIE: /to the principal's office. Well I could tell you a thing or two about him too.

CINDY: *(Refrain she has heard many times.)* A janitor sees a lot of business.

BONNIE: That's right.

CINDY: You only want bread.

BONNIE: No I don't. It's your father's birthday ain't it?

CINDY: Yes.

BONNIE: Well I never was to town to get him somethin' so I want to make him a special sandwich. *(Puts her purse down.)* Fifty-six cents won't buy what I want. Did he leave any money for the egg woman?

CINDY gets a tin down.

CINDY: Five dollars.

BONNIE: That'll be enough.

CINDY: It's for the egg woman isn't it?

BONNIE: *(Mocking.)* Isn't it? Yes but it is his birthday. I want to make him a lobster sandwich.

CINDY: *(Quickly.)* You can't eat lobster.

BONNIE   Well it ain't for me is it? Don't I know them doctors told me I can't eat lobster? Lobster sandwich is nothin'. I ate the most beautiful lobster in my dream last night. I was a girl again and my pappy was takin' me out for supper. Just him and me. Not Laura-Lee or Betty-Lou. Me and him.

CINDY: Mom I got to get going…

BONNIE   I won't tell you the whole dream, about how fancy the restaurant was, just like on *Another World* and I was wearing my pretty party dress. Pappy sat me down at the table with him and smiled a beautiful white smile. And he says to me "Eat all you want my Bonny Bonnie." Wasn't that clever? I look down at my plate and it's piled high with steaming lobster meat and there's this little gold pot of melted butter beside my plate. Then he reaches over and picks up a bit of lobster, dips it in the butter and starts bringing it to my mouth. His hands are soft and white, like he never fished a day in his life. But it is his lobster from his boat fixed at this fancy restaurant just for me. I open my mouth and he puts it in. The smell and the butter on my tongue, some of it dribbles down my chin. He wipes it with a white cloth napkin. Then that brother of yours starts in wailin' about the cramps and it's all gone. Pappy was so real.

CINDY: Can I go Mom?

BONNIE: A can of lobster and a loaf of bread. Make sure it is none of his old bread either.

ENID enters tries the light and this time it works.

CINDY: What if he asks about the slip?

BONNIE: Tell him what Bill say. "If he didn't charge exorbitant prices he would be paid on time." Tell him Bill'll be up on Friday.

CINDY goes out.

Scene Seven

ZOË, wearing music earphones, enters as CINDY goes out. ENID watches her.

ENID: Hello. That was you I saw crawling in the window.

ZOË removes her headphones.

I said it looks like you ripped your jeans there crawling through the window.

ZOË: That's not what you said.

They take a measure of each other.

ENID: I'm Enid. I knew your Grammie many years ago.

ZOË: Where is she anyway?

ENID: She went upstairs to find her purse.

ZOË: *(Sighs heavily.)*

ENID: Ruth doesn't seem…well.

ZOË: We wouldn't be here if she was "well."

ENID: Ahhh. You like the house, do you?

ZOË: No.

ENID: It used to be the house of the village. Teenagers sneak in for drinking parties in the winter when it is too cold behind the dunes. I have to keep my eye on it.

ZOË: *(Coolly.)* Right. Mom wants to know where the closest LCBO is.

ENID: The what?

ZOË: The booze store. The place where people by al-co-hol.

                They study each other.

ENID: You have to go to town for that.

ZOË: God there is NOTHING here. What do people do for fun, drown themselves?

ENID: Well they don't do it for fun but lots of ones have been lost at sea.

ZOË: Gram has a picture of you in a bathing suit.

ENID: I don't look like that now.

ZOË: No you don't. Did Gram like KILL someone.

ENID: No! Good Lord... NO!

ZOË: She did something bad.

ENID: Ruthie never did anything terrible like that. It's not in her nature.

ZOË: Something happened, she told me she would tell me when I got old enough.

ENID: Did she? I am not saying things didn't happen. Anyways things that seemed so terrible to us back then nowadays people go on talk shows to brag about it.

ZOË: I told Mom Gram doesn't want to be here.

ENID: Ruthie said that did she?

ZOË: I know it.

ENID: She didn't have the easiest time growing up.

ZOË: Why?

ENID: It was a long time ago now I don't know if I should say.

ZOË Guess I'll ask people until someone says.

ENID: I guess I saw a lot more than anyone. Her father drank, that made it hard. Her mother wasn't easy— she had this voice on to her. After Bobby was born with problems—he was a Mongoloid—it was like Ruthie was dead to her. Ruthie and I had awful good times though—girls together.

ZOË shouts up the stairs.

ZOË: Peg, there is a person here.

Scene Eight

SHERI and DAVID are sleeping. RUTH bends over DAVID reaching out to touch him.

RUTH: Frankie? Frankie!

SHERI sits up. She looks at RUTH but she sees BUDDY.

SHERI: Noooo. Don't don't.

>*DAVID pulls SHERI down beside him.*

He's on the boat David. He's grabbing hold of you.

DAVID: It's a dream Sher.

SHERI: I feel—him. He's there.

>*She looks again directly at RUTH.*

DAVID: Watch me.

>*DAVID reaches out beside RUTH mimes grabbing Buddy and dropping him over the side of the boat/ bed.*

Buddy is sinking…sinking…sinking…gone— under the sea.

RUTH: Yes yes Me Frankie? Me.

SHERI: He's there David.

DAVID: Shhhh go to sleep chere Sheri.

>*SHERI winds her body around his as if to hold him back from BUDDY's hand, to hold him back from the gaping black hole of the sea.*

RUTH: Please me that one me.

>*RUTH mimics his actions.*

Sleep sleep sea.

Scene Nine

>*PEG comes down the stairs.*

PEG: Hello? —Oh I was expecting a Mr…

>*Checks the cut sheet for name.*

ZOË: Mom she is not Mr. Real Estate Loser—she's Gram's bathing suit Enid.

ZOË strikes a bathing beauty pose.

ENID: Oh dear.

PEG: Enid! A friend—a friend of Mom's.

ZOË groans, sensing all is lost.

ENID: That's right we was girls together.

PEG: I'm her daughter Peg and you've met Zoë my daughter. Has she seen you? Zoë where's Gram?

ENID: Yes we had a little visit. She went upstairs.

PEG: She recognized you!

ENID: Well maybe not rait off...

PEG: But she did know you.

ENID: Yes, yes.

PEG: Oh that is so great. See Zoë.

PEG calls up the stairs.

Mom! Mom!

ZOË: She's on planet purse.

PEG: *(Shouting.)* Mom your purse is in the car, remember?

ZOË snorts.

Go get her.

ZOË: She won't do anything for me when she is looking for her fucking purse!

PEG: Zoë, not acceptable. Mom is having a little trouble with her memory.

ZOË: Dementia. Hello!

PEG Don't be rude. All right leave her for a bit. She is

changing so much becoming a sweet old lady. She used to have this voice.

ENID: Her mother had a voice.

PEG: She told us the little place at the end of the village was the home place.

ENID: The one with no paint—yes.

PEG: She shampoos with toothpaste, but she remembered that house. She said it looks the same, didn't she Zoë?

ENID: Well it has changed some.

PEG: The flower beds made her sad. *(Remembering suddenly.)* You would have known my father.

ENID: Your father?

PEG: Frankie.

ENID: Yes...yes I knew him.

PEG   Do you see a resemblance?

ZOË: Ahhhhh what does it matter? I don't want to look like you or Dan.

          PEG decides not to start things.

PEG: Everything looks so familiar like the landscape has been transmitted in my genes.

ZOË: It's familiar because Gram makes us look at the drawings all the time.

ENID: I watched her draw a good many of those.

PEG: Not Mom my father drew those.

ENID: Frankie? No. He use to say "Oh, I can draw I can draw water/

PEG: /from a well." That's what Mom said about herself.

ZOË: She drew them. It was our secret.

ENID: That's what she meant by don't say it. I shouldn't've said.

PEG: Why would she...lie? She told me so little. I want to put together the puzzle of her past. God knows I am losing the present with her.

ZOË: But we aren't staying. The real estate person isn't coming.

ENID: They said they would send someone out, did they?

PEG: Yes of course.

ENID: (*Looking doubtful on that.*) I turned the power on for you anyways.

PEG: Thank-you.

ENID: My Jack caretook this house for thirty years. I know this house.

PEG: Maybe he could answer my questions.

ENID: He's passed. Emphysema. He only smoked half a pack a day. Some of the ones that smoke two are still going.

ZOË laughs out loud.

PEG: How long has the house been empty?

ENID: It's been a few years now since Carol moved out west to live with her girls. She's with one, one month then shoved on to the other the next then back again—homeless really. Those girls were always odd. Carol's husband died out there in the ditch. Too crippled to push himself out of that little bit of water there was at the bottom of it.

PEG: Didn't anyone see him, didn't she hear him?

ENID: He couldn't talk—he'd had the stroke years before.

PEG: That's horrible.

ENID: Yes. Course he had led Carol quite a merry dance before that. After he use to sit in that front room there and watch the road. I got so use to seeing him sitting there sometimes when I look out my kitchen window I swear I see him still.

ZOË: Yewwwwww. Haunted by a stroke ghost.

PEG: Zoë there isn't a ghost.

ENID: No…no—my own fancy is all.

                    RUTH calling from the upstairs.

RUTH   Peg! Peg! Now. Now!

PEG: There's Mom's old *bossy* voice.

RUTH: Frankie! FRANKIE!

PEG: Sometimes she forgets he is gone.

ZOË: Dead.

                    ENID reacts.

PEG: I wanted to bring her to the place she was happy.

ZOË: She wasn't happy here. *(To ENID.)* Tell her!

PEG: Zoë enough!

ENID: She never told me she wasn't happy.

ZOË: You said her father/

ENID: /was like lots of ones. He liked a drink. Her and I had good times though.

RUTH: *(Off.)* Peg. PEG?

PEG:	Coming Mom.
ENID:	I only came across to see if you had any questions.
	She gets ready to leave.
	RUTH laughs.
	It was built sound this house. If you need anything I'm just a shout. Bring Ruthie over before you go.
PEG:	I will. Thank you.
	ENID leaves.
RUTH:	*(Off.)* Peg.
PEG:	Get her purse so I can settle her down.
ZOË:	She said that Gram's father was a stinking drunk.
PEG:	*(Disbelieving.)* Enid said that.
ZOË:	And she said her brother was Mongol...or something.
PEG:	Down Syndrome? No, Gram said he was a little slow.
ZOË:	She said her mother was "verbally abusive."
PEG:	Zoë please.
ZOË	You heard her she said she had a voice.
PEG:	You have a voice. I heard her say that Gram and she had good times. Go and get Gram's purse.
ZOË:	No.
PEG:	Zoë, now.
ZOË:	No, you take me to the airport now.
PEG:	I don't have money for a plane ticket to Toronto. And you forget, you've burnt your bridges with

your father. Go get your grandmother's purse.

ZOË: If you make me stay here I'll drown myself.

PEG   Well if you must but first get the purse.

ZOË goes out.

Shit. "BUZZZZZZ" wrong come back bad mother.

PEG goes up the stairs.

Scene Ten

Upstairs bedroom. PEG enters the bedroom where SHERI and DAVID are sleeping. RUTH is looking out of the window.

PEG: Here I am at last.

RUTH: Water's coming look in yes.

PEG: Still pretty far out. I can just make out the line of waves.

DAVID moves in his sleep.

RUTH: *(Turns at the sound.)* Frankie.

PEG: No. Frankie's dead.

RUTH pauses stopped by utter grief.

I'm sorry. Don't cry. You know that, you know he's dead.

RUTH calms a bit looking down at the sleeping couple.

Yes you know it.

PEG kisses her mother.

RUTH: Like this. Like this. Whole. Like this, whole.

She clasps her hands trying to show PEG.

PEG: There's no hole in the bed, Mom. Did you know
            that woman downstairs?

RUTH: Whole.

PEG: Enid. Mom? Did you recognize Enid?

            *RUTH gets her sketch book searching until she finds
            ENID.*

PEG   Yes, I can see her looks. She told me that you did
            these drawings. You.

            RUTH hides the book behind her back.

            I'm not going to take it away from you. Mom it's
            OK. OK. This room has a nice feel doesn't it? Is this
            the room want? You can see most of the village
            from here. The houses are such colours. Like their
            fishing boats. Enid will come to see you every day
            and you'll have friends, women friends. Did you
            ever wish you had never left the home place? If you
            stayed there never would have been the accident.`

RUTH: Peggy…

PEG: Even after Dad died, so young to be on your own
            with a baby, why didn't you come home? Wouldn't
            it have been easier? Don't get upset, you're tired,
            I'm sorry.

RUTH: I have…

PEG: You have…what?

            RUTH taps her head shakes it.

            Take your time.

RUTH: The mother one…she one…

PEG: Your one—yes?

RUTH: Something…

           She touches her head.

PEG: You told me she was a quiet woman. Enid said she
           had a voice.

RUTH: In here. In here.

PEG: She sent you one-dollar bills to give me for
           Christmas. She never came to visit because she had
           to take care of Bobby.

RUTH: · That one push push. Push she.

PEG: Bobby pushed you? Had a sibling thing going on
           did you? You said he was slow—Enid told Zoë
           Mongoloid did Bobby have Down Syndrome?

RUTH: *(Taps head.)* Comes in and in and in and that way
           that way every…thing…gone *(Desolate.)* gone.

PEG: Sounds like you've got the ocean in there. Forget
           about it Mom we don't need to know.

RUTH: Don't you one get this.

PEG: Lie down Mom, rest your head.

           RUTH sadly points at DAVID.

RUTH: Not Frankie. Not my bed.

PEG: It belongs to whoever buys the house. Lie down.

           RUTH lies on the bed.

RUTH: He smells like the sea. Frankie's skin leaks salt.

PEG: You can say the most beautiful things.

           Sound of a musical truck horn outside.

ZOË: Pegggggggg! PEEEEEEEEGGGGGG?

PEG:	Oh god.
RUTH:	What's that *(She attempts to hum it.)*?
PEG:	It's Zoë bellowing as usual.
RUTH:	No.
ZOË:	PEEEGGGGGGGGGGG.
	Musical truck horn.
PEG:	Yes. Just rest for a bit.
	PEG leaves.

Scene Eleven

Sound of musical truck horn. SHERI sits up in bed.

SHERI:	Is that Jerry?
DAVID:	He's parked his truck at the end of the drive.
SHERI:	His lights off?
DAVID:	Yeah. Trou du Chu. Asshole.
SHERI:	I saw him talking to you at the dance.
DAVID:	He was pretty drunk.
SHERI:	What'd he say?

Sound of the musical horn. DAVID opens the window and leans out.

DAVID: Hey Jer. You're going to wake up my son. Go sleep it off.

The truck starts and slowly pulls away. Sound Trou du Chu.

SHERI: What did he say to you?

DAVID: I told him when he wakes up with a hangover the size of the Fundy Basin he can think of me waking up to the prettiest girl on the whole damn shore.

SHERI: He don't think you got a prize with me.

DAVID: Sure he does.

SHERI: Jer and them all thought Buddy was such a great guy. I bet they all told you marrying me was bad luck. A fisherman's widow.

DAVID: They did that.

SHERI: I knew they would.

DAVID: I told them, "Tu seras mon porte-bonheur."

SHERI: What?

DAVID: Tu seras mon porte-bonheur. Try it, Tu seras…

SHERI: Tu…tu…ser…

DAVID: Seras.

SHERI   I can't… I can't…what does it mean?

DAVID   Tu seras mon porte-bonheur. Sheri, tu seras mon porte-bonheur. You are going to be my charm.

Scene Twelve

ZOË sits in the widow's walk. The floor is littered with many different kinds of alcohol bottles. She sits staring at the bottles. PEG comes up the stairs. She sees RUTH's purse.

PEG: Zoë? Zoë. You were calling me.

ZOË: Never mind now.

PEG: I was with Gram.

ZOË: Too bad. Too late.

              PEG tries the door.

PEG: May I come in?

ZOË: Would "No you can't" stop you?

PEG: I'd like to see the view from up there.

ZOË: GOD. Can't you leave me alone?

PEG: You wanted… All right. I'll leave you alone. If "you vant to be alone." Zoë? Zoë?

ZOË: What? What?

PEG: I'm going to Enid's to call the agent. Listen for Gram. *(Pause.)* Zoë.

ZOË: What?

PEG: What? What did I just ask you to do?

ZOË: God.

              PEG waits.

              I'll listen OK!

Scene Thirteen

              CAROL is moving around getting ready to go.

CAROL: Enid said she saw Marsha over at the corner. Wouldn't have known her if she hadn't heard she was home. That's the way they dress in the city I guess. Good of her to come over.

              LUD struggles to speak.

              I say it's good for her to stay with you while her mother and I go to town.

LUD begins to breathe harshly. He seems to be having trouble catching his breath. His head rolls as he struggles.

Easy. Slow down. Breathe. You're all right. That don't scare me anymore. That don't keep me home now.

LUD recovers quickly.

LUD: NNNoooh.

CAROL: You sure? Don't you ask her to take you to the bathroom. She don't want to see an old man's butt.

MARSHA knocks on the door.

CAROL: It's open Marsha.

Enter MARSHA, 17. She is dressed in a very confrontational way. 1980s disowned youth— leather, punk hair, etc.

MARSHA: Hi.

CAROL: Enid was right. I wouldn't have picked you right out in a crowd of strangers.

MARSHA: Yeah, I guess.

LUD stamps his foot once.

CAROL: No she's not forgetting you. Say hi to Marsha.

LUD stamps his foot.

You can do better than that.

LUD: K-K-K-

CAROL: Not K-K-K. You know who this is?

MARSHA: So he knows stuff, right?

CAROL: Doctors don't know how much he remembers. Can't say too much…few words.

LUD:	K-K-K-
CAROL:	Me?
LUD:	NNNoooh.
CAROL:	NNNoooh is one of them. Say "hi", "hi".
LUD:	*(Stamp, Stamp, Stamp, Stamp.)*
CAROL:	He's in a mood with me.
	LUD reaches for pipe.
	No more pipe until bedtime.
MARSHA:	Mom said he can't walk.
CAROL:	Oh he shuffles along. Cane on his good side and me on the other. He won't need to get up.
LUD:	MMM-mmm.
CAROL:	Maybe he knows you. You know this girl? Use to help you out in the barn. Do you remember? No?
MARSHA:	I do.
CAROL:	Good someone does, I guess.
MARSHA:	Mom said you can pick her up anytime.
CAROL:	All right. Our appointments are at three. *(CAROL holds out her long ponytail.)* Told me when he married me, if I cut my hair he would leave me. Good many nights on the farm I sat in that kitchen with scissors in hand.
MARSHA:	I brought him something.
CAROL:	Orange Lifesavers. He always had a pocket full of those.
MARSHA:	I remember. *(She puts the roll on the table.)*

CAROL: Now he's had his soup and he's been to the
            bathroom. He won't have to go again until I get
            home. If he does have to go just lead him to the door
            and help him off with his braces. He can't get those
            on his own. But he can manage all right, in there.
            I go in and help him but *(To him.)* you can manage
            yourself. Do you have to go?

            LUD shakes his head and grins.

            Good. Well, see you soon.

            CAROL goes out.

MARSHA: Everything will be OK.

LUD: Pppee ppppeeee.

MARSHA: Drop dead.

Scene Fourteen

            *ZOË enters space looking for RUTH. RUTH is
            agitated.*

RUTH: Drop dead drop dead drop dead drop dead. Ppppp
            drop dead!

ZOË: Gram…shhh shhh Gram.

RUTH: Drop dead. That one yes drop dead dead dead.

ZOË: Gram don't say drop dead. It's not nice.

RUTH: That one there…that one wants to…to… I don't
            know it.

ZOË   Gram listen, listen to me.

            RUTH touches ZOË's hair.

RUTH: Don't change it green.

ZOË: No one does green hair anymore.

RUTH:	DROP dead. Drop DEAD.
ZOË	Gram don't say… ahhh…bananas. Don't say it.
RUTH:	Don't say it. Don't say…
ZOË:	Bananas. Oops.
RUTH:	Oh you said…you said… *(Giggles.)*

RUTH touches ZOË's face and kisses her.

ZOË:	Where are your shoes Gram? Gram. Where are your shoes?

ZOË is hopeful that RUTH is present.

RUTH:	Brown one ones.

ZOË sighs. She sees her shoes but does not point them out.

ZOË	Gram please. Let me whisper. *(ZOË leans into her Grandmother's ear.)* Want to go for a drive? In the car. Gram?

RUTH goes to the window.

RUTH:	That there. Go there.
ZOË:	To the smelly disgusting wharf? Sure. (NOT!) OK, no shoes no car.
RUTH:	No shoes, no car.
ZOË:	Ah, here they are!
RUTH:	Noooo. Wedding shoes. Bride shoes. Shhh. Shhh.
ZOË:	Wedding shoes are white. These are…not white.
RUTH:	I want brown one ones.
ZOË:	If I find them will you come with me in the car?
RUTH:	Yes. My ones. Brown.

ZOË makes a great show of looking for the shoes.

ZOË: Here we are! Found at last! Let's put on your shoes.

RUTH: NO! My ones.

ZOË looks at her. Takes off her own shoes and put on the flats. She walks up and down the room several times while RUTH watches darkly.

ZOË: Nice. I like them. My new shoes.

RUTH looks away.

Yeah! I love these shoes. I'm never taking them off.

RUTH: Not brown.

ZOË: I know I love blue shoes. Great with jeans or dresses. Flats too. I love flats. These are the BEST!

RUTH: Blue.

ZOË Do you like blue eyes, blue sky, blue water, blue bottles, blue bells, blueberries, blue bird...

RUTH: Blue shoes.

ZOË: You want my old stinky sneakers?

RUTH: No.

ZOË OK. Let's not talk about shoes.

RUTH Talk about shoes.

ZOË Gram do you want to go in the car to the smelly disgusting wharf?

ZOË holds up a credit card.

I have gas money.

RUTH protects the bank money.

Not your book money.

RUTH: Not going talk about shoes.

ZOË: People will think I'm old enough to drive because I'm driving with you.

RUTH: Blue.

               RUTH tries to touch the shoes.

ZOË: Ah ah ah. Want to try them on?

RUTH: No! Brown one ones!

ZOË: Gram! If I get the fucking brown one ones will you come in the car with me?

RUTH: Brown, brown, brown.

               ZOË slips on her sneakers.

ZOË: OK. Stay here, Gram. I'll get the brown shoes and the fucking car keys. Shhh secret don't tell Peg. Gram, shhhh.

               ZOË leaves.

Scene Fifteen

               DAVID gets up and begins to dress. RUTH watches and then begins to strip off down to her slip, bra and panty hose. For one brief moment they seem in the same time staring across the years. Glow of DAVID's cigarette, he sits on the edge of the bed, dressed in jeans and a sweater. SHERI comes in.

SHERI: He's sleeping. You ain't goin' out are ya?

DAVID: I've been getting 150 lbs. to a tub all week.

SHERI: They'll be there tomorrow.

               Sound of a musical truck horn going by.

DAVID: There go Jer and the boys. You want a new house. I got to catch some fishes.

SHERI: I've changed my mind.

DAVID: You want to live here? Have Enid on our doorstep every five minutes, snooping around?

SHERI: There are houses for sale in the village. Let's buy one and fix it up the way we want.

DAVID: You said you don't like living in other people's houses. You said, "A person living in this house can't enjoy a lobster sandwich."

SHERI: Some houses ain't got stories.

DAVID: That you know of. It won't be so bad living next to Mom and Dad.

SHERI: I don't want to know what the sea is like when you're out on it. The day Buddy went over I could see the water changin', getting' black with the wind and the waves startin' to spray up over the wharf. I don't want to be always staring out the window watchin' for the water to turn on us.

DAVID: It doesn't turn on us. The sea isn't good or evil. It just is. Like God.

SHERI   Jerry and them, they got to fish but you don't.

DAVID: A classroom full of grade eight students is more terrifying than any blow out there.

SHERI: What about Buddy?

DAVID: You have to learn not to be scared of the water, Sher.

SHERI: Da's boat was caught in a terrible storm when Mom was carrying me. It put the fright in me.

DAVID: No.

SHERI: It's true. Things can happen to babies inside because of what their mothers did. There was this woman, stained her apron doing up preserves?

When her baby was born he had a birthmark on his back exactly the same as that stain from them plums.

DAVID: Was he scared of plums?

SHERI: You can laugh but I hate the water since always. I saw Lud drown a little brown puppy one day. He filled a bag with sand and tied it to the puppy's collar and threw him off the end of the wharf. I didn't know what he was doing until he threw it. I started screaming and crying, yelling at Lud to jump in and get it but I couldn't get out of the truck 'cause I was afraid the wharf would sink. Lud heard me and came over. Told me the pup had tore into his chickens. Said once a pup gets a taste of chicken blood there ain't no cure. Sneak them anytime he can. He gave me some candy but I wouldn't take it. I told him I wished someone would tie a bag of sand around his neck and throw him off the wharf.

DAVID: You said that to Lud?

SHERI: Yeah. I never go to the wharf.

DAVID: Come out with me tonight.

SHERI: The boys will say you're crazy letting a woman on your boat.

DAVID: Were you ever in Bud's boat?

SHERI: No.

DAVID: And he drowned anyway. I'll teach you to fish, to love it out there too.

SHERI: I can't.

DAVID: Come one.

SHERI: I can't leave Garyleigh.

DAVID: Bring him.

SHERI:	A three-year-old on a boat, in the middle of the night. Now I know you're crazy.

SHERI: A three-year-old on a boat, in the middle of the night. Now I know you're crazy.

DAVID: All right tomorrow afternoon. You and Garyleigh, a tour around the harbour.

SHERI: Garyleigh'll climb over the side, knowing him.

DAVID: We'll tie him, you too, if you want.

SHERI: I'll be scared enough.

DAVID: I'll be there. OK? I know to Jer and them I'm just un boiteux, a crip(ple).

SHERI: You went to college.

DAVID: A college education is nothing. For a guy like me it isn't anything but a reminder of what I'm not. I'm a good fisherman Sher.

SHERI: You promised to be a good husband.

He kisses her.

DAVID: Oui, Madame Melanson, je promet. Come out with me. We've got to teach our kids not to be scared.

SHERI: Maybe. If the water ain't black.

Scene Sixteen

ZOË is digging through PEG's bag for the keys. PEG comes in from outside.

PEG: I've left another message.

ZOË: I need the car keys. Gram wants her brown one ones.

PEG: Is she in a state?

ZOË: Sort of. The keys Peg?

PEG: In my bag.

> *ZOË looks again.*

ZOË: Why don't you go for a walk on the beach? I'll stay with Gram.

PEG: After the agent comes.

ZOË: The keys aren't here.

PEG: If we're lucky she's forgotten all about her...

> *RUTH enters from the stairs. She is wearing only a bra, pantyhose and half-slip.*

MOTHER!

ZOË: Gram, not now.

PEG: Where's your DRESS?

RUTH: Wet. Me get all Wet.

PEG: You wet yourself?

> *RUTH looks confused.*

RUTH: Wet.

PEG: Oh Christ I'm dealing with a two-year-old.

ZOË: Peg, the car keys?

RUTH: Fucking car keys.

> *RUTH moves towards the door.*

PEG: You know how she picks up that language. Mom where are you going?

RUTH: Don't tell, the beach.

PEG: You can't go outside like that. The neighbours will see you.

ZOË: What do you care? You were naked!

PEG: Not that now Zoë, Christ. Go get her dress! Did you
            go to the bathroom at the garage like I told you? Or
            did you twiddle your thumbs in there?

ZOË: Peg, the car keys!

RUTH: Fucking car keys. Shhhh. Money for gas. Shhhh.

PEG: What is she talking about?

RUTH: Money book?

            RUTH starts to get quite distressed.

PEG: Stop blithering about that goddamn money book.

ZOË: I'll get your money book Gram.

            ZOË goes up the stairs.

RUTH: Peg. Peg. Ten dollars for the bus?

PEG: We drove down. We DROVE down. WE DROVE
            DOWN.

RUTH: That woman took my money book. Not old bread.
            The thingy not the fish…[lobster]

PEG: Are your pantyhose wet? Oh just take them off.

RUTH: Don't push push me.

            ZOË comes in carrying RUTH's dress

ZOË: Why are you pushing her?

PEG: I wasn't. You know that's her thing she says when
            she's upset with me.

ZOË: Everything is dry. I think she made a mistake.
            (Giggles.) You didn't make a mistake Gram.

PEG: Oh really. Why would she take her clothes off?

ZOË: You didn't pee Gram. *(Hooting.)*

RUTH laughs.

PEG: Stop it Zoë. Calm down. If you don't stop she will wet herself.

ZOË: Here's your money book Gram.

RUTH: Gas money shhhh.

PEG Take your dress in that room and get dressed.

RUTH: No water. Wet.

PEG: Goddamn it. Now Mother NOW, I said now. NOW!

RUTH like a chastened child goes to bedroom.

ZOË: You don't have to yell at her.

PEG: That was not yelling.

ZOË: *(Mimics the tension-filled but guarded voice.)* That's how you yell. She was better off in that home.

PEG: One. I can't afford it. Two. They were sedating her all of the time.

ZOË: So she wouldn't run away.

PEG So she would be easy they turned her into a drooling old shell. She's sick but she's still in there.

Lights up on LUD and MARSHA. MARSHA sits at his feet.

ZOË: Gram runs away, that's what she does. She'll run away from here.

PEG: I know and these people will know where she belongs.

ZOË: That old guy died in the yard.

PEG: That won't happen.

ZOË: I'll run away and you won't find me…if you bother to look.

PEG: Stop punishing me Zoë. It was a tiny student art show.

ZOË: It was published in the paper. Everyone saw you.

PEG: I didn't know the critic would choose to print his painting.

ZOË: "Corporate wife undressed."

PEG: That was supposed to be funny.

ZOË: I heard what Dad said.

PEG: He can't feel violated because I take my clothes off.

ZOË: You brought him to my party. Dad talked to him.

PEG: I've told you we were not in a relationship then.

ZOË: Then. You've ruined Dad's life.

PEG: This is far too complex for this moment. OK?

ZOË: You love someone or you don't.

PEG: If you've noticed Dad has put his life back together rather quickly.

ZOË: Your fault.

PEG: My fault too I suppose if you were arrested for driving without a license—which is really what you wanted the car keys for, right…I'm not stupid.

ZOË: Being here is stupid.

PEG: This is the safe place for Gram.

ZOË: She doesn't want to be here.

PEG: She has been asking to come home for months.

ZOË:	No, she's been asking to go to the water, the ocean. Maybe she wanted to go to Hawaii.
PEG:	Don't be silly.
ZOË:	She never came home before, did she?
PEG:	She never could afford to.
ZOË:	No. Her mother did a terrible thing to her.
PEG:	What?
ZOË:	I don't know.
PEG:	Because it didn't happen. This will be a good place for us.
ZOË:	NOT for ME, NOT FOR ME!
PEG:	Look out there. Tell me what you see.
ZOË:	Fog.
PEG:	What do you see?
ZOË:	No city, no friends, no life.
PEG:	You'll make nice friends I promise. There are women, like Enid, who will watch out for Gram.
MARSHA:	(*Off.*) Round and round the garden.
PEG:	Zoë, I haven't any choice. I can't live in Toronto without a job. Gram can't be left alone. I can't afford to have someone come in. It's the only way. Here I can have a studio-gallery right out there in the barn.
ZOË:	Why can't I decide for me?
PEG:	This is a tourist route. I can sell pottery here, give classes to the locals. I've thought this out carefully.
ZOË:	No, you didn't think about me. I promise I promise. No more drinking.

PEG: You're right, no more drinking.

MARSHA: *(Off.)* Round and round the garden... *(Stops.)*

ZOË: You can't control me. EVER! I HATE YOU! I hate Gram. I hate Daddy and that bitch. I'll live on the streets. I will. I will.

                RUTH hears ZOË shouting and she is affected by it. ZOË leaves.

PEG: *(Beat.)* I wish I could start over with her.

Scene Seventeen

                MARSHA is staring at LUD.

MARSHA: Round and round the garden...

LUD: K-k-k-k-

MARSHA: Carol isn't here.

LUD   K-k-k-k-k-

MARSHA: She'll be back. Are you there, Lud, "Uncle Luddie"? Do you know who I am? Fuck, do you know who you are?

                Round and round the garden

                Runs the Teddy Bear

                One-step Two-step

                I'll tickle you under there.

LUD: K-k-k-k-

                MARSHA takes out a can of neon orange paint. She shakes the can, sprays it in the air over his head.

                STAMP STAMP STAMP.

RUTH comes out fully dressed.

RUTH: There is something wrong…that little girl. *(RUTH makes the motion of spraying the paint in the air.)* Psssst. Psssst.

PEG: Here's your book money.

RUTH: Peg. The one hate hate.

PEG: No, no she's angry with me. She loves her Gram. Sometimes I look at Zoë and I think all my years of inaction wired her with rage. There she is. From here she looks 12…an angry 12. Remember I knew she was going to be a girl. I was certain…this connection… Daughter.

RUTH: Shave his belly with the rusty razor. Shave his belly with a rusty razor.

PEG: What's this? You sing too? Bringing you home is good. *(PEG sings.)* Shave his belly with a rusty razor. Early in the morning.

RUTH: *(Dreamy.)* Nothing to shave. Brown and bare as a nut above his belt. Below…there…white sweet white…tasting of the sea.

PEG: Mom!

RUTH: *(Startled.)* Don't, don't tell Daddy.

PEG: I should say not. She hopes I'll go back to Dan.

RUTH: I don't know him why you married him I don't know it.

PEG: He had that measuring up voice I heard from you all my life.

RUTH Oh dear dear, oh.

PEG: Hello are you really here, Mom?

RUTH: Hello.

PEG: I tried hard in that old life Mom. Tried hard but failed. Dan did too. Funny I can admit that now. There were so many terrible words between us. Miles of bitter words enough to collect a divorce. What I didn't see was that those words travelled between us through the body of Zoë. Even the ones we made sure she didn't hear even the ones we kept inside.

    RUTH opens the book and slowly looks through.

    Why didn't you tell me it was you who did these?

RUTH: Me. Me.

PEG: I know. I wish you hadn't given up drawing. Maybe I would have gone to art school years ago. Dan said, "People your age go to Art Schools to have affairs." It is annoying to think he gets to think he's right as usual. But I didn't. I went to see if I was any good, if all those years of pottery classes added up to something important.

    He was, is, the art history T.A. The very first class he asked to paint me. I told him no. Every day he'd stop me, "Peg the beautiful, let me paint you." I'd tell him, "Women my age aren't beautiful." One day I showed him the varicose vein on my thigh and I said See I am not beautiful and right there in the student coffee shop he leaned over and kissed it. I got in the car to drive home even though I had two more classes, but on the way home, at the light there was this biker beside my car. He had a huge beard.

    BONNIE gathering up things to make sandwiches. It is a ritual. Bowl, spoon, can opener, Miracle Whip.

And leather pants, oh I thought he looks like he is bad news. But at that moment he reached down and touched the bare ankle of the woman on the back of his bike. He touched her skin like it was a rare find, like my thigh had just been kissed, and I thought Yes.

RUTH echoes the Yes sweetly.

I want that. I want that in my life. I turned around, drove to his studio. I took off my clothes and he painted.

RUTH: Yes.

PEG: Now look at us. Bombs are exploding in the middle of our world. All I can think is, this way I can start over with Zoë again.

RUTH: Want water. Peg?

Knock on the door.

PEG: Maybe Zoë's right, maybe it was the ocean you wanted not home. Were you happy here?

ENID arriving at the door.

Someone from your past, it's like an omen, a good sign, right Ruthie?

Knock on the door.

ENID: Hello, Bonnie? It's Enid.

BONNIE sneaks back to the bedroom.

RUTH: Where did that girl go?

PEG: She'll be back. Zoë will have come around.

Scene Eighteen

> *ENID opens door and comes in. She has two dozen eggs with her.*

ENID: Bonnie? Cindy said you're up.

> *BONNIE reappears.*

BONNIE: Enid, you're out early.

ENID: Early bird catches the worm. I left Jack wanting his tea.

BONNIE: We don't need no eggs.

ENID: No?

BONNIE: Good till Monday anyway.

ENID: Bill said yesterday you were low to out. Said he'd settle up with me today.

BONNIE: Never said.

ENID: Two dozen and settle up.

BONNIE: Alls he said was the eggs didn't seem as good. The yolk seemed funny in 'em. I said you wouldn't sell us eggs that had froze.

ENID: He never said nothin' to me about froze eggs.

BONNIE: I told him they was just fine.

> *She goes and picks up the tin.*

> Noooo…nothin' here. Seems to me he did have a ten dollar bill in his wallet for you…now that I think.

ENID: I told him it ain't more than five.

BONNIE   He was thinkin' of paying ahead like. I'm sure he said this ten dollar bill is Enid's.

ENID: But he didn't leave it?

BONNIE: His head too filled with big words to remember anything.

ENID: But the way he said…

BONNIE: Tommy will run it to you after school. You be home today or would tomorrow be better?

ENID: I'll plan to be home.

BONNIE: You might as well leave those eggs, save you lugging 'em. And if you give 'em to Tommy he likely smash 'em gettin' 'em home.

ENID: No, I…

BONNIE: We'll be paid quite a bit ahead.

ENID: I'll keep them since you have some to last you to Monday.

                 BONNIE rubs her legs.

ENID: How are your legs?

BONNIE: Terrible through the night.

ENID: Aspirin help?

BONNIE: I wish it did.

ENID: Your mother suffered from legs, didn't she?

BONNIE: Good many times I had to rub the back of her legs with mineral oil. Sometimes I cried myself to sleep my arms pained me so.

ENID: Well Jack's waiting for his tea.

BONNIE: I had a dream about Pappy last night. Realer than real.

ENID: Some dreams are.

BONNIE: He was white and shinin'. Like an angel.

ENID: An angel?

BONNIE: A beautiful dream, Enid.

ENID: My mother said when your father wasn't thumping The Book he was thumping somebody's head.

BONNIE: Eh?

ENID: She said he was a hard man to cross.

BONNIE: He looked like an angel.

ENID: Now don't get upset. He raised his family—I know that—lots of men did less.

BONNIE: He called me his Bonny Bonnie and fed me lobster with his soft white fingers.

ENID: Good thing it was only a dream. That stuff is poison to you.

BONNIE: That's what that doctor say but I don't' believe it myself. I think I just got a bad one that time.

ENID: Well I told Jack I wouldn't be more than a minute.

BONNIE: You have one small pleasure and somebody got to take it from ya.

ENID: The cat will be wanting in for his breakfast.

BONNIE: On a day like this it's something awful being alone, Enid.

ENID: Here take a dozen. I know you don't need them but it would save me a trip. We all have hard days Bonnie.

            CINDY enters with a brown paper grocery bag.

BONNIE: Did you get the bread?

CINDY: Yes.

BONNIE: You didn't see nothin' of a ten dollar bill, did yah?

CINDY: No.

BONNIE: Bill had ten dollars for eggs for Enid. He never give it to you?

ENID: Funny him saying like.

BONNIE: I'll send Tommy over after school.

              BONNIE rubs her head.

ENID: Don't let her think 'bout her pappy. Don't want to start your head.

BONNIE: No...

ENID: We all have our days.

              ENID goes out.

BONNIE   Why in hell did you tell her I was up?

Scene Nineteen

              RUTH is enjoying the last few bites of the Oh Henry bar.

PEG   Ten months ago you were just a little forgetful, I was blissfully in school, and Zoë was doing OK, I thought. I remember opening night of our art show thinking, "After eighteen years I'm finally living the life I've wanted so badly."

              I had thought going to art school after all these years would show Zoë determination and courage. Oh God, standing at the end of that hospital bed I knew that all I had showed her all of her life was self-denial and anger.

Everywhere I go I see mothers and daughters together. I watch them. I am obsessed with watching them. The other day in Loblaws I saw this mother with her little girl. The girl was sick and her nose was running and she had this whiny draining voice. The mother was so angry and tired and the daughter knocked something over. The mother's voice. God. I wanted to go to her and say to her Whatever your daughter has done it is nothing. But your voice, that tone, she will die of it and you will have to live with knowing that it came from you.

But the faces that wake me up in the night are the mothers and daughters I see laughing and smiling together. Those faces, oh mother. It is unbearable. I think did you ever love me like that? My god, did I ever make Zoë feel that loved? No, all I have done is laid harsh words on her skin and now they are etched on her bones.

Sorry. Sorry. I don't want to make you sad.

We're in this big storm aren't we? Hurricane Ruth... Peg...Zoë. You feel it don't you?

RUTH: Yes.

PEG: Yes, I think you do.

Scene Twenty

Several hours later. Dusk. RUTH sits alone with her bank book. PEG comes running in, in a panic. She is carrying ZOË's CD player and also her sneakers.

PEG: Mom I found this on the shore, and her sneakers floating in the water. Have you seen Zoë?

RUTH shakes head. PEG puts the sneakers and CD player on the table. Quickly checks the downstairs bedroom.

Zoë. Zoë?

PEG runs upstairs.

SHERI is in bed. In the widow's walk a single spotlight. SHERI sits up slowly.

SHERI: David. *(Panic.)* David?

PEG enters upstairs bedroom.

Buddy! *(Fearful.)* Buddy!

PEG: Zoë? Zoë?

Lights out sharply in widow's walk.

Zoë?

Scene Twenty-One

MARSHA What do you want to play today? Pull the finger. Pull the finger. *(She slowly spray paints his left hand.)* Do you remember me?

LUD: Ppppppeee.

MARSHA: If I knew for sure you were in there.

LUD: Ppppeee.

MARSHA: *(Loudly.)* LUD?

LUD doesn't respond.

Scene Twenty-Two

The lighthouse light flashes around the space. Thumping on the door of the widow's walk.

PEG: Zoë. *(Pounding.)* Zoë! Answer me. GODDAMIT. Are you there?

PEG pushes door up. Empty. She sees all the bottles on the floor.

PEG: Oh my god!

She leaves the space. The lighthouse light stops revolving.

End of Act I.

Act II

Scene One

> *LUD is moaning in the chair.*

MARSHA: You were supposed to understand [what I'm doing to you].

> *LUD rolls his head. Gasping.*

Shit. What's wrong with you?

> *LUD begins to breathe harshly. He appears to be having some sort of an attack.*

Are you just a helpless baby? Are you? FUCK. Is this like a stroke or something, like another stroke or something?

LUD: P-p-p-p-

MARSHA: Take it easy, take it easy. P yeah yeah ppp what. Pee? For fuck sake is that what you mean?

> *LUD subsides.*

LUD Pppee.

> *MARSHA hesitates. LUD breathing funny again.*

MARSHA OK, OK, OK.

> *LUD stops.*

Cane on good side me on the other.

> *Walks over and hands him the cane. Moves behind and lifts him out of the chair. Supports him as he shuffles over to the door.*

LUD: K-k-k-k-

MARSHA: She's not here. I'll help you with these.

> *She removes one suspender and as she is removing the other he speaks.*

LUD: K-k-k-iss.

> *MARSHA freezes. Then like a coil unsprung she moves grabbing the cane away. She moves as if to swing it at his head but uses it to push him backwards through the door. She follows him in.*

Scene Two

> *PEG comes down the stairs to main space.*

PEG: Zoë? She's not here. Mom, did you see her?

RUTH: YES.

PEG: Where is she?

RUTH: The one that one you have to get, get.

PEG: I know. Where did she go?

> *RUTH copies MARSHA's movement with the cane.*

PEG: Mom, what are you doing?

RUTH: Something bad. Something bad.

PEG: What did she say?

RUTH: The one needs help.

> *MARSHA rushes out.*

PEG: Who...who do you mean? Zoë?

RUTH:	Out the door. Gone. Go get her.
PEG:	When? When? Just now? Just now?
RUTH:	Yes yes just now out the door out the door. Kiss… kiss…out the door out the door. Just now just now… Listen. Listen to her.
PEG:	Listen to Zoë…isn't that all I do? Stay here. Mom stay, I'll be right back.

PEG goes out the door.

RUTH:	Who's going to help now?

Scene Three

SHERI lights a smoke. Sound of a car pulling in.

SHERI:	Oh Christ.

Knocking.

Come in Beulah.

BEULAH:	Where's Gram's boy?
SHERI:	Garyleigh is sleeping. We didn't get home until after midnight.
BEULAH:	I told you I'd keep him. I brought him a present.

She takes a 5x7 picture frame from her purse.

SHERI:	I got pictures of Buddy.
BEULAH:	This one is Garyleigh's. For his dresser. Where's hims bank.

SHERI gets the tin and gives it to her. BEULAH drops in coins.

He went out this morning, did he?

SHERI: Yeah.

BEULAH: Not much of a honeymoon.

SHERI: It's been good fishin' all week. David wants to save up so we can start building this fall.

BEULAH: Where you gonna get a lot?

SHERI: His father give us a piece next to him.

BEULAH: Some rocky on that point. Buddy always knew he was gonna get the home place.

SHERI: When you was done with it.

BEULAH: Some people give up their place and move into a trailer and they're never happy again. Buddy didn't want me to be unhappy.

SHERI: [Right.]

BEULAH: I went to the cemetery yesterday.

SHERI: Yeah?

BEULAH: Even if his body ain't there it's a place to go.

                SHERI takes a puff, blows smoke out, and puts cigarette out.

                Margie was tellin' me the other day about a woman who smoked and her baby was born with a harelip.

SHERI: I've been up since five o'clock. I needed a smoke.

BEULAH: Shouldn't be sick this late. I ain't never heard of anyone still sick in their sixth month.

SHERI: I'm only three months.

BEULAH: Seems like it's been goin' on a lot longer than that. Garyleigh will be sick staying up so late. He didn't need to go to the wedding.

SHERI: We wanted him there.

BEULAH: He said he did, did he?

SHERI: Yes, Beulah.

BEULAH: Well, at least he's saying it now.

SHERI: You don't think David wants Garyleigh?

BEULAH: I never said that. But another man's boy is a big
            responsibility and maybe he wasn't thinking about
            that. Things happened so fast between you and
            him.

SHERI: Now they happened fast. First you was claiming
            I'm six months pregnant, now you're saying we got
            married too quick.

BEULAH: I'm just worried about my grandson.

SHERI: I wouldn't marry someone that wasn't good to my
            son.

BEULAH: Could he come and visit his Grammy for the day?

SHERI: I ain't goin' to wake him up, Beulah.

BEULAH: I know Buddy never went to college but he was a
            good provider.

SHERI: If I could get the money before he went to the Red
            Lion with Jerry and them.

BEULAH: You can't tell me he didn't keep you good. He give
            me one hundred dollars every mother's day since
            he was sixteen years old. One hundred dollars.

SHERI: That was Buddy.

BEULAH: Well it was Buddy. And he loved that boy too. He
            was as good as good could be with that boy. And it
            breaks me to know…to know Garyleigh ain't even
            gonna remember his real father.

SHERI: You'll tell him what a great guy his daddy was.

BEULAH: I will. What breaks me is what he's gonna hear from some.

SHERI: Who?

BEULAH: I'm not naming no names.

SHERI: You mean me?

BEULAH: I don't want Garyleigh growing up thinking his father was any less than any other man.

SHERI lights up a cigarette, puts it out again.

SHERI: He wasn't less than Jerry or Cecil.

BEULAH: No, he wasn't. Or David either when you come down to it.

SHERI: That's what you want to think.

BEULAH: Is that what you're gonna tell Bud's boy? 'Cause if you're gonna be saying things like that I want you to give Garyleigh to me.

SHERI: What?

BEULAH: You heard me Sheri. I want him to come live with us.

SHERI: So you can bring him up like you brought up Buddy?

BEULAH: Yes.

SHERI: No. I don't want him brung up to be drinking when he's thirteen or dropping out of school in Grade Nine.

BEULAH: Well maybe I could of done better but I know one thing, you can't raise a soft boy.

SHERI: He wasn't soft but he was lazy. Too lazy to get out of bed to go fishing half the days.

BEULAH: I said Buddy didn't have a fancy education but he was a good provider. He give me one hundred dollars…

SHERI: Yeah and I didn't have a thing to wear to town.

BEULAH: If you wanted fancy clothes you should have got a job in the fish plant.

SHERI: I just wanted a decent place to live. Five years in this dump. Freezing cold in the winter. Your precious son let your grandson wake up to a freezing cold house because he was too friggin' lazy to chop wood for the kitchen stove. Well, his son ain't goin' be cold this winter. Dave's goin' to built us a new house. We won't have to wait for someone to die before we can get a place to fix up.

BEULAH: If he sticks around. Everyone knows he thinks he's better that everyone else because he went to college. But he ain't no better. He's fishing like all the other boys and he got trapped just like lots of ones.

SHERI: I didn't trap Buddy.

BEULAH: Not with a baby. When you're a seventeen-year-old boy there are other traps.

SHERI: Is this what you're going to be tellin' Garyleigh?

BEULAH: I'll tell him what I know.

SHERI: If you get to see him.

BEULAH: You can't stop me. Just remember you might need Buddy's family some day. David *(Emphasizing the French pronunciation.)* Melanson might go up here to school and find himself a nice French teacher.

Then where will you be? Don't think his family is gonna let you in their door 'cause they ain't. Happy to see him shed of ya. Then the home place will look pretty damn good to you and don't you think it won't.

SHERI: Go home Beulah. Before I say something you don't want to hear.

BEULAH: Don't you get to high and mighty girl. That's all I got to say.

SHERI: Don't you worry Beulah. I will never ask for your help.

BEULAH: The home place might look like a palace to you some day.

BEULAH leaves. SHERI goes upstairs.

Scene Four

LUD is standing in the doorway with his pants down around his knees. His hair is painted orange. ENID enters.

ENID: Carol? Luddie? Are you here? *(Aghast.)* Oh good Lord, Luddie, what are you doin'? How did you get into paint?

LUD: NNNNOOOOOH.

ENID: Where's Carol? Carol? Carol? Get these pants up man.

The front of his pants are painted orange. Just as she gets them up he topples over.

Oh Lord. You hurt eh?

CAROL comes in, her head covered with the scarf.

CAROL: Where's the girl? Where's Marsha?

LUD lies on the floor. Moans.

ENID: There's no Marsha. Just him. Naked for all the world to see and looking like one of those ugly trolls the kids play with. How did he do that to himself?

CAROL picks up can of paint.

CAROL: Maybe Jack'll hire you to paint the house in the spring eh?

ENID: I don't know how you'll get that off him.

CAROL: It'll come off eventually.

ENID: I can help you get him up.

CAROL: I don't need your help. All them years ago it might have made a difference.

ENID: I wasn't the only one you asked.

CAROL: No you weren't.

ENID leaves. CAROL takes her coat off. Walks over and stares down at LUD.

Scene Five

RUTH and PEG are huddled in the widow's walk peering out. The lighthouse light is going.

PEG: They've turned on the light for her.

RUTH: Where's the girl?

PEG   Someone maybe saw "someone" walking out to the island. It's cut off until low tide. Three more hours they said.

RUTH: Yes. Where's the girl?

PEG: Don't keep asking me that. I don't know I don't

	know. Surely to god she's not walking to Toronto in her bare feet.
RUTH:	The one can't get up.
PEG:	What one?
RUTH:	The one there can't get up.
PEG:	Watch the light Mom. Look for Zoë.
RUTH:	I don't want you to catch this. *(Taps her head.)*
PEG	The widow's walk. What would they call a room where mothers wait for their daughters?

Scene Six

                         BONNIE is getting ready to make the sandwiches.

BONNIE:	I said, why'd you tell Enid I was up?
CINDY:	She asked.
BONNIE:	*(Mocking.)* "The early bird catches the worm." Holds up the eggs over her head smiling. They do. *(Chuckles.)* Did you get it?
CINDY:	I was thirty-two cents short.
BONNIE:	He put it on the slip?
CINDY:	Said he ain't putting no more on the slip.
BONNIE:	He didn't give it to ya because you didn't have thirty-two cents?
CINDY:	He says I have to bring it up before school. He won't put another cent on the slip until we pay what we owe.
BONNIE:	Oh is that what the bastard said?
CINDY:	*(Sniffs.)*

BONNIE: He give you a hard time?

              CINDY nods.

              Oh I can hear him too.

              *Acts out the scene between the storekeeper and his
              wife. Pulls herself upright, begins stroking her neck
              with two fingers and staring in a horrified manner
              at CINDY.*

              (In STAN's voice.) "Lobster! *(Shrieks.)* Lobster!"
              Strokes neck faster "What them that can't afford
              bologna will buy, eh Jessie?"

              *Now BONNIE strikes the pose of the wife. Makes
              clicking sound with her tongue, shakes her head,
              dour.*

              (In STAN's voice.) "I suppose next they'll be ordering
              the caviar."

              *Now BONNIE is the wife. Titters. She returns to
              being herself.*

              One day he's gonna rub that old Adam's apple so
              hard pop right out of his mouth, eh? Then what old
              Jessie gonna stare at all day?

              *BONNIE mimics JESSIE, head following the
              movement of his Adam's apple.*

              "Yes, Stan, yes Stan, yes Stan."

              CINDY has been smiling. Now she giggles out loud.

              The old coot, the old bastard.

CINDY: I got to go so I can get to the corner.

BONNIE: When five o'clock comes and he don't have his
              thirty-two cents he's gonna put it on the slip.

CINDY: But he said that I had to bring it before school...

BONNIE: You leave old, "can't put another cent on the slip" till after school.

           BONNIE opens can to make sandwich.

           While you was gone I was thinking about Pappy. He never gave me nothin' like in that dream... nothin'. My bonny Bonnie, it was "you" or "girl" or worse...a lot worse. It was Laura-Lee this or Betty-Lou that but Bonnie was only fit to wipe his fishy, greasy, dirty hands on. Yes, that's all. Never had a day of happiness in his house. Not a day. Not my birthday, or Christmas or any day. Never once happy in his house. And Tommy is just like him. Yes he is. Got his mean eyes like his very soul is shining through.

CINDY: I'll make the sandwiches, Mom. You go back to bed.

BONNIE: I feel like it. In November it's all I'm good for but I got to try and give some happiness to my family. Do special things for Bill and you and Tommy. But not for Tom today. Get me the peanut butter. Get it. He don't deserve no lobster treatin' me the way he did. Don't you go givin' him your sandwiches either. It's what Pappy deserves.

           She makes up the peanut butter sandwich quickly. CINDY puts it in a bread bag. BONNIE lovingly stirs the lobster. She picks up the can, runs her finger around it and brings her finger towards her mouth.

CINDY: *(Panic.)* Don't.

BONNIE: A lick of juice ain't going to kill me Cindy. *(Pause. Wipes her finger on her night-dress.)* Enid thinks I probably just got a bad one that time. Does it look pale to you?

CINDY: No.

BONNIE: Never seen such pale lookin' lobster. Get the *catsup*

	will ya? *(BONNIE shakes some in.)* There. There! That's better. Ain't it pretty?
CINDY:	Yeah. Mom I got five minutes to get there. I don't want to get in trouble.
BONNIE:	Taste it.
CINDY:	No.
BONNIE:	I want to know if it's good. *(Spoons some into CINDY's mouth.)* Is it good?
CINDY:	Yeah.
BONNIE:	Well do you want a sandwich or not?
CINDY:	It's good. It's good.

BONNIE quickly does up a sandwich, drops it in a bag and hands it to CINDY.

BONNIE:	Well git goin'!
CINDY:	What about Dad's?
BONNIE:	Tell him I'll bring it up.
CINDY:	You don't like going out.
BONNIE	Bill asked me this morning to go up and visit him at the school. Said he'd take me out for an ice cream sundae after. He said "Go for a walk today, woman. Get some of those spider webs blowed off ya." He said, "Get a quantity of the arachnids' filaments ventilated off your anatomy."

I feel like a walk today. I do. What a birthday surprise for our Dad, eh?

Now you're gonna be late Missy.

| CINDY: | I'll wait. |

BONNIE: And get sent to old man Spence's office? You know I'm gonna walk up and give that old bastard his thirty-two cents.

CINDY: Will you?

BONNIE: Don't see why not. The school is halfway there ain't it? You're gonna be late.

CINDY: I'll tell Dad you're coming.

BONNIE: If you want to spoil the surprise.

CINDY: *(Unsure.)* OK.

BONNIE: Let him think we forgot all about him. Let him think nobody remembers his birthday.

CINDY goes out.

Scene Seven

ENID is sitting next to RUTH.

ENID: You was at the house she said. I said you did go by the home place today. Americans bought it. Pretty little place now.

RUTH: The flower beds there, those ones there.

ENID: There beside home place? Yes. Yes she does. That's right…peonies…red ones. You'll see them if you're here in June. They grow good there on that side.

RUTH: Red?

ENID: Beautiful ones.

RUTH: Those beds there hurt.

ENID: Why dear? Why?

RUTH: Hurts me so, Enid.

ENID: It wasn't a pretty place back then was it? Outside or in. Don't think about it. *(ENID opens purse.)* Look I brought you something.

Takes out a couple of sheets of paper and a pencil.

Brought you something, eh?

RUTH shows no interest.

ENID: You ain't forgotten how? You ain't forgotten how to draw. Don't want to? I'll leave it on the table you can draw me a picture later.

RUTH looks out of the window.

RUTH: Lights.

ENID: Ya, them's the flashlights. Zoë's lost her way. The whole fire department is out looking for her. This is what a community is, eh? I'd say to Jack…a man gets burnt out, the neighbours help raise him back up…a child gets lost in the woods…everyone turns out to search. Don't hear of that in the city.

RUTH: Listen.

ENID listens.

BONNIE: Let him think no one is happy he was born or cares enough to give his soul one small pleasure. *(Stares at the sandwich.)* Just one. *(Puts the sandwich in a bag.)* I feel as though I could walk up there today. I used to love to get out of the house and walk. Walk the roads. Pappy stop me "you girl", no worse, a lot worse. "You get your fat ass home."

ENID: No. Don't hear nothin'. Told Peg Frank died, eh? Just as good, maybe. You had a good life afterwards, though, didn't you? You never wrote me or nothing. *(Pause.)* I wasn't the one that told your mother you was pregnant. Ruthie did you think I told her? Maybe she guessed. My father always said he could tell when a girl was pregnant just by looking in her eyes.

As ENID talks RUTH gets ready to draw but just as she's set to begin she re-adjusts everything.

We used to love to walk the beach didn't we, eh? Back then I'd wake up in the night and listen to the water. In the night the tide would change. I use to think the tide could make every day fresh, white like the sand. Then it seemed like one winter all those rocks came in but maybe it happened gradual...anyways they won't be washed away. No... No...can't be you see because the rocks don't come in, the sand is washed away exposing the rocks. I look out my window now all I see is rocks.

RUTH: That old man can't get up.

ENID: Who dear? Are you thinking about old Lud drowning out there? What goes around comes around I hate to say. Carol came to me one time when their girls were little, asked me to take them. They was living out on the farm then. Not a word why, just would I take the both of them. How could I do that? Take a man's children? I think about her asking me that. Plenty of ones had it hard. They all did. I saw a lot in this house. I know what some of them said about me.

RUTH: They all did.

ENID: That's right. Jack would say a man's home is a man's...it was never none of our affair. *(Pause.)* I did think that too once.

RUTH gives ENID the bank money.

RUTH: Help Peg. Money book.

RUTH opens the bank book.

ENID: You want to help do you?

RUTH:	YES!
ENID:	I ask because some just take… *(Looks at balance.)* Oh my landy, $37.29?
RUTH:	Mine help.

She leads ENID to the window.

ENID:	What is it dear?
RUTH:	Beach gone.
ENID:	It'll be back in the morning when the water's low.

RUTH takes off her shoes, begins to undress.

What are you doing, Ruthie?

RUTH:	Beach. Water. OK OK.
ENID:	No. You've got to stay here. You can't go traipsing down to the beach now, it's almost one in the morning. Ruth, you have to wait for Zoë.
RUTH:	Zoë.
ENID:	YES. Terrible thing if she comes back and her Gram is gone. You got to stay here for Zoë. Zoë wants her Gram to wait.

RUTH suddenly goes to the table. She begins to draw.

Draw us a nice picture. *(Pause.)* He came back. Did she ever write you that? Months later Frankie came back looking for you. Your mother wouldn't tell him where you was at. No sir. He came to me. Jack and I was just married. Frankie asked me to find out where you was…figgered she would tell me. Maybe she would have. Alls I could think was how his wife must be feeling.

I kept thinking…what if Jack did it with some girl

and left me for her. Left me stuck with babies like that. Ruthie? I was a wife too, eh?

RUTH sits back and claps hands. ENID walks over and looks at the paper.

Ain't you going to draw a picture?

RUTH   Water.

ENID: You didn't draw nothin' yet.

RUTH   *(Firmly.)* Water.

ENID: My eyes is bad but they ain't that bad. I see it. A little rock or something, under the water is it?

RUTH: Me. Done. Done.

ENID: Done is it? I'll put it on my fridge door. Brighten my door, eh? *(ENID tucks it into her pocket.)* Do you know what I've been saying, Ruthie? Frank came back.

RUTH: That girl is lost.

ENID: Zoë will be back. I'll go over and get you a blanket so you can have a lay down. I'll stay with you so you can sleep. I don't mind waiting tonight. Can't think why I ever did. Your mother was awful sorry for it in the end. I know she wished awful bad she could have made it up to you.

ENID leaves.

RUTH: That girl is lost.

BONNIE: I had ways of sneakin' out. The boys with cars, the boys already fishing would slow down...drive beside me. "You got something for me Bonnie?" "I love you Bonnie." And I loved riding around in their smoky cars. One night Bill dropped me off and Pappy met me at the door sayin' terrible things. Terrible things that weren't true so I ran out, caught

Bill at the corner and made them all true. After we was done Bill said, "You don't need to be parading the road no more." And there it was, all gone.

BONNIE unwraps a sandwich. Takes it into the bedroom with her.

RUTH: One voice in a house asking...no one comes to help the one out.

Scene Eight

SHERI, with a life preserver on, comes in begins packing a picnic into a cardboard box. Knock at the door. Louder knocking. ENID enters.

ENID: Sheri it's me dear. What are you doing?

SHERI: Making a picnic.

ENID: Jack sent me over.

SHERI: Did you see Garyleigh out there pretending his sandbox is a boat? Knows how to start a one. Got it memorized. Tells me a hundred times a day.

ENID: He said you was taking him down to the wharf.

SHERI: I'm packing a picnic that's a surprise. He won't be expecting a picnic.

ENID: Jack's been listening to the CB all morning. Sheri, there's been some trouble they're saying.

SHERI: *(Pause.)* I said I would be too scared. He'll be some surprised to see me on the wharf.

ENID: I said, "Jack I don't want to be the one again..."

SHERI: Ain't the water blue today? I've never seen it so blue.

ENID: That's what I said. I said, "Men go down in storms. You expect that..."

SHERI: The boats are in Enid. I've got to get down to the wharf.

ENID: They found *The Journey* an hour ago. More. Looping crazy circles like. Nobody could raise him on the set so Jer pulled to thinking he fell asleep at the wheel. They couldn't see nothin' so Cec jumped on board. David was gone. Jer figures the trawl got wound around his bad leg, pulled him over the side.

SHERI: Buddy!

ENID: Not Buddy, dear, David. David's been lost. I hated to be the one.

              SHERI pushes past to get out the door.

              Now you're not going to the wharf, dear? Wait here. The Coast Guard's out there looking. What about Garyleigh? Should I take him to Beulah? Sheri?

SHERI: NO.

ENID: Alright dear, alright. Maybe they'll find him.

              SHERI leaves.

              Oh dear heart, twice a widow, who will have you now? I'll take him to Beulah. He's got to go somewheres.

Scene Nine

              RUTH removes her shoes carefully. She moves towards the door with determination. The sound of gut wrenching sobs. Lights up on widow's walk. It is unclear where they are coming from but all the women characters pause for just one second as if hearing the depth of the grief backwards and forward in time. PEG is sobbing in the way one does when completely alone and enveloped in grief. RUTH is stopped by the sound. She turns back. She stands at the stairs listening.

RUTH: Peg? Help Peg?

Scene Ten

SHERI strides down the front of the stage. Pulls the canvas off the ship's wheel.

SHERI: Leave me be.

The engine grinds but doesn't start.

You think I don't know my way out of this harbour? I have spent my life watching boats going in and out. Da's and Buddy's and…this one.

She grinds the engine again.

I see you Jerry. What's the matter Jer? Want to do it on the deck? Can't even wait a week this time before you come sniffing around. Trou du chu. You TROU DU CHU. That's French for asshole, ASSHOLE.

The engine starts. SHERI opens the engine wide.

Scene Eleven

LUD is on the floor. CAROL is standing near him.

CAROL Got your wind yet?

CAROL slowly and deliberately slips off scarf to reveal very short hair.

Like it? Eh? I asked you if you like my hair now?

LUD: NNNOOOOHHHH.

RUTH: All those wrongs.

CAROL: I do. I wish Marsha was here to see it. I wish our girls could see my hair. Well, it don't change the past.

Scene Twelve

PEG: Mom, I feel so frightened. *(PEG indicates her centre.)* I have this pain, this loss, here.

                RUTH puts her hands to her head in a mirror of CAROL's action.

RUTH: All the anger.

SHERI: *(Over the engine.)* DAAAAAAVVVVVIIIIIDDDDD.

PEG: No I'm afraid. What if she's drinking...ill?

                The engine cuts out. Sound of the water against the side of the boat.

SHERI: DAVID?

PEG: What if she got in a car with someone?

RUTH: LISTEN!!!

SHERI: David you've got to fight him. David you've got to fight him. You made promises to me. Buddy you listen to me. You let him go. I seen you in the night. I knew what you was up to, too. *(Pause.)* Buddy you listen. You give me reason, you know you give me reason. That day I saw the water turning black...black and the wind coming up I wished... When Enid told me your boat had gone down I thought there, the sea knows what my life was like with Buddy. It seen the bruises that nobody, not Jer or Enid or especially Beulah looked at. I thought, maybe the sea can be good. I wished you lost. Damn you, Buddy, I did. I DID. David you promised you would be a good husband. David. What about Magi? What about Garyleigh? What's going to happen to us now? David. *(Sees him)* David? DAVID!!

                PEG moves into action mode.

PEG: They've been looking for hours.

RUTH: That one is all right, now. The girl is coming back, the daughter.

PEG: I'm so tired I can't think straight. When Enid gets back we'll...I don't know. I don't know.

            ZOË runs in, throws herself weeping in her grandmother's lap. PEG moves forward but stops. ENID comes in quietly.

            Where was she?

ENID: Tommy that drives the tow truck for the garage found her going out the road to the highway. They went to a dune party up the way.

PEG: All this time?

ENID: He said she told him she was eighteen.

PEG: Were you hurt? Zoë?

            RUTH strokes ZOË's hair.

RUTH: Don't don't colour it into green.

ZOË: No one... *(Does that anymore.)*

RUTH: Don't turn it it in on you. You.

PEG: Answer me, were you hurt?

ZOË: No.

            RUTH goes into the bedroom door, watching BONNIE.

PEG: What were you doing at that party?

ZOË: God, that's all you care about too. Did Zoë drink?

PEG: You've been gone ten hours!

ZOË: I can find drinking friends here too. *(ZOË blows in her mother's face.)* Disappointed.

RUTH: Don't let one eat...Enid. ENID.

ENID: Who dear?

                BONNIE takes a bite of the sandwich.

RUTH: No eat the one sandwich.

                RUTH enters BONNIE's bedroom and watches over her.

BONNIE: It tastes so good to me.

PEG: She's beat. She's not making any sense.

ZOË: She doesn't want to be here. She's worse.

PEG: You disappearing has made her worse.

RUTH: Enid. No one hears. Listen to be hungry.

ZOË: Gram you don't want to be here, do you?

                BONNIE settles back and is still.

PEG: Don't ask her that at 2:30 in the morning.

ZOË: Gram tell me you don't tell secret.

RUTH: Don't tell secret.

PEG: Please don't get her started.

ZOË: Why don't you want to know?

PEG: Her secret isn't horrible Zoë. She was most likely pregnant with me when she married my father.

RUTH: NO Frankie Frankie gone gone.

PEG: Yes he's gone. No more sad Mom.

RUTH: Enid. Enid. Say. Say. Frankie.

ENID: You want me to say do you? Frankie was already married. He had a wife and children over on the Cape.

RUTH: Where is that girl gone?

ZOË: I'm here Gram.

PEG: But they were in Toronto together. He was struck one winter's day walking home from work.

ENID: No, no my dear, he went back to the Cape before she run away. He came back for your mother…months later Frankie came looking for her. He would have gone to Toronto if Ruthie's mother or I had told him where she was.

PEG: There was no marriage? No accident? Nothing she told me when I was growing up is true?

ENID: Was you scared to tell your mother Ruthie?

RUTH: Git up git dressed.

ENID: That voice gives me chills Ruthie.

RUTH: Don't tell your Daddy. No! Push push push out the door out the door…one dollars warm from her apron. Git the bus git out. SLUT!

PEG: MOM.

ENID: All those years she made out you'd run off. When it was her who had turned her own back on you.

RUTH: Don't catch this this Peg.

PEG: Too late mother, you've given it to me. All those stories, your happy childhood…my father… erased…lies.

ENID: Not lies. I don't know what to call them things to make people feel better. Not lies.

PEG: All these years you put this made-up father between us. All of your stories untold for some untrue stories that were suppose to what? Make me happy?

ENID: I guess she told those things so you would have something to hold on to. It must have hurt her to give up drawing. To give it over like that.

PEG: It hurt me! We could have shared—a passion. She gave me this driving need to marry into being safe. SAFE. Now I'm not married and I've got two lives depending on me and the one place I thought would be safe was horrible for her.

ENID: Her and I had good times!

RUTH: (*Laboured but urgently.*) I want to eat eat that sandwich Peg.

PEG: Jesus mother please try. I can't stand it. It's too hard.

RUTH: (*Pause.*) Peg say it. It live. Want that, my life.

        PEG *puts her face in her hands.* RUTH *touches* PEG's *head.*

PEG: Mom you repeat the worst things at the wrong time.

RUTH: Peg want. Peg

PEG: It isn't a question of what I want Mom, it' what I can afford.

ZOË: I want to go…

RUTH: No no shhhsh. Say say. Peg you you…

PEG: I want to finish school. I want work and art and life.

ZOË: Your school is in Toronto.

PEG   We can't afford Toronto.

> *RUTH begins searching her purse. She takes out her bank book.*

Yes Mom, your $37.29. I'll be able to make a down payment on a house in Forrest Hills.

> *RUTH walks away. She goes to BONNIE's room.*

RUTH: Enid.

ENID: Yes, dear?

RUTH: Like this like this. Done.

ENID: What are you thinking about Ruthie?

> *RUTH searches through the pocket of ENID's sweater.*

RUTH: Water?

ENID: What's the matter dear? You want your picture back? You can have it dear.

RUTH: Like me Ruthie one like. It tastes good to me. Bag of sand. Here here (*Motions around her neck.*) Over the side. Little brown one puppy. The ditch one… right out there. Out there. The lobster one one. (*She motions it over her head, points to the "rock."*) Ruthie. Me.

ENID: (*Understanding.*) Oh my dear.

PEG: What?

ENID: Are you drowned in this picture?

RUTH: Water one.

> *Motions it over her head.*

PEG: Mother oh my…is that what you're planning?

RUTH: Help that daughter one.

ZOË: Gram Grammie no. I'm sorry.

PEG: That's why you wanted the water, that's why you wanted to come home?

ZOË: It's because of me because I'm so mad at her.

PEG: Zoë that's not…

> *ZOË runs up to the second storey.*

See, who do I run to? Who do I try to rescue?

ENID: I know what Ruthie would say.

PEG: But…

ENID: Ruthie and I have got something to talk about don't we?

> *PEG goes up the stairs. CINDY enters and crosses to BONNIE's bedroom.*

Scene Thirteen

ENID: You held that thought all these many months, all that long drive down here, all this long day and night. See that buoy light out there? One time it saved a man's life. Yes it did. They'd found his boat empty circling around. They was sure he was lost but Sheri found him. She went out on his boat by herself and found David hangin' on to that buoy for dear life.

> *CINDY gets her mother's purse and takes out a compact.*

I often wondered over the years if Jack would have come back for me or gone after me to bring me back. Your mother wanted to see you awful bad. She was sorry Ruth. I know it.

RUTH: Me be water.

CINDY holds the compact up to her mother's nose.

ENID: No No. You don't want Peg walking into the sea on Zoë someday when things is hard. The thing is mothers can't do that. It teaches their kids how to do it.

I don't know what it's like to have children myself. Cats was all we had. One time I lost a cat and I cried my eyes out. Jack loved that cat too but he lost patience with me. "Woman," he said, "it's just a cat." I knew that. I was crying because I knew that was going to be my life, crying over a dead cat.

CINDY closes the compact and runs out of the house.

Lots of ones in this house had it hard. Over the years I saw things. I saw a lot. It takes up my mind. I wish I'd done things different. Ruthie? I'd do it different now. Would you stay with me for a bit Ruthie? While Peg and Zoë get things up there straightened around. You and I can walk on the beach every day.

RUTH: Walk the beach.

ENID: We loved to do that didn't we? Oh my landy I'd love to be that girl again.

Scene Fourteen

ZOË lays across the bed crying.

PEG: It wasn't because of you Zoë. Your Gram is sick, confused. She wants what she thinks is best for us.

ZOË: If we all got lost from each other we would be better off.

PEG: Do you think so?

ZOË: I don't know.

PEG: Look, kids go through phases.

ZOË: Parents go through midlife crises.

PEG: Don't trivialize.

ZOË: Like yeah!

PEG: OK, but this drinking is stupid.

ZOË: You do stupid nude things.

PEG: It is not the same thing. Drinking is destructive. You will ruin your life.

ZOË: Like that painting ruined yours.

PEG: No, it released me.

ZOË: You're released mother bye bye.

PEG: No, what happened never had anything to do with my mothering you.

ZOË: Yes right.

PEG: I know you're rebelling because I…

ZOË: God Peg, not everything that happens in my life is because of you.

PEG: OK. I will try to know that. *(Pause.)* What am I supposed to do?

ZOË: Go back to school.

PEG: You hated that.

ZOË: I do hate it. But we'll be in Toronto.

PEG: I don't know how I can make it work there.

ZOË: God, Gram did and she was alone and pregnant.

PEG: I feel so sad. She built a wall between us, a stupid story about a father and now there is this wall of dementia. I think I did that to you too. Only the wall was…

ZOË: Mad. You were always mad at me.

PEG: No…not at you.

ZOË: You yelled at me.

PEG: I'm sorry.

ZOË: I'll sleep on a pull-out couch.

PEG: What?

ZOË: If we can live in Toronto.

PEG: A pull-out couch? Why we'll be so poor we'll have pull-out cardboard boxes.

ZOË: Mom!

PEG: Oh God, that is the nicest thing you have said to me in a long time. Time to get your grandmother to bed. Come on.

         They go down the stairs.

         Time for bed Mom?

RUTH: No.

PEG: Oh God.

ENID: Peg dear, I'd like to have Ruthie to stay with me. I'd like that an awful lot.

PEG: Well that's so kind but we need to get back to Toronto. Sorry Mom, we'll have to have a rest and then head home.

RUTH: Peg home.

PEG: Where that is I don't exactly know yet.

ENID: I'd like to have her stay with me for a little while. For awhile like. You will be doing me a favour, been lonesome since Jack died. Since Jack died I can call the place my own.

PEG: Mom's a lot of care, Enid.

ENID: Would you stay with me, Ruthie?

RUTH: Yes.

PEG: Some days she's not very good.

ENID: Oh, I think we can manage. Can't we Ruthie?

RUTH: We're old enough.

             ENID and she laugh.

PEG: Mom, would you stay with Enid?

RUTH: Yes.

PEG: Mom. Do you want to stay here, down here with Enid?

ENID: I'd like to have you stay, Ruthie, see those peonies next to your home place in June. It would be good for you to see that bed in bloom.

RUTH: Yes. See. Frankie he..he… *(Smiles.)*

ENID: came back…Yes.

RUTH: Yes. *(Smiles.)*

             RUTH goes out.

PEG: Zoë get her to the car…

ZOË: *(Calling out.)* Shotgun, Gram!

             ZOË leaves.

PEG: All right, Enid. If you're sure you can manage. It would give me time to get set up.

ENID: Us girls will walk the beach every day.

PEG: Oh, God…

ENID: No, no I won't let go of her.

PEG: There's a house there on the point. I didn't notice it before. Someone has turned on all the lights.

ENID: The one with windows in the whole front. Yes. Magi says David and Garyleigh get up three o'clock, same as if they was going out, same as if there was still fish in the sea.

PEG: It's been a long night. I don't have a key to lock up.

ENID: I do. Well I like to keep one. Check it once in awhile. It's too bad it's empty. It was the house of the village.

PEG: It has a very pretty view.

Lights go down as they prepare to leave.

The End.